Mom & Me

10 Super Stories About Moms

hachette
INDIA

First published in 2010 by Hachette India
An Hachette UK company

www.hachetteindia.com

SRD

ISBN: 978-93-5009-227-9

Hachette India
612/614 (6th Floor), Time Tower
MG Road, Sector 28, Gurgaon 122001, India

Typset in Minion 11/13.7 by
Eleven Arts, New Delhi

Printed and bound in India by
Manipal Technologies Limited, Manipal

FSC www.fsc.org
MIX
Paper from responsible sources
FSC™ C043100

CONTENTS

THE COVER-UP

RANJIT LAL

'Hello, my dears, I have a surprise for you . . .' Old Mrs. Kapur smiled at Lalit and Sudha, who had popped their heads around the door of her Animal Rescue Centre, as they did every day on their way back home from school.

Lalit was twelve, a tough, stocky chap with a 'bristle cut', and Sudha, his best friend, was ten-and-a-half: a small wiry girl with a snub nose and stubborn chin and three missing front teeth, and one hell of a tough cookie. They were neighbours in the colony just down the road from the Centre and had been friends ever since they could remember. Well, ever since they had 'jointly' bashed up the Bhatnagar bullies a couple of years ago.

Actually, Sudha had rescued Lalit from getting pasted by the twins.

He'd been flat on his back, with the twins sitting on his chest, hammering away when she had sailed into battle screaming, 'two against one isn't fair!'—and emptied a pail of ice-cold water (it was December) over them, and then whacked them left and right on their ears and cheeks as they gasped and spluttered. Taken aback, they had fled howling, clutching their stinging ears and cheeks, while Lalit gasped like a goldfish and then bounded up and roared off in pursuit.

He was man enough to return and briefly nod his thanks to her.

'Thanks,' he said, 'I was about to flatten them . . .'

'Yeah, yeah, I know,' she grinned, 'Thought I'd save you the trouble!'

'I'm Lalit, I live in B8 . . .'

'I'm Sudha from B4 . . .'

'Hi . . .' Diffidently, he held out his hand.

'Hi!' Her bony fingers squashed his palm.

'Good grip!' he complimented.

'I know. Do you know someone left a huge bull mastiff at Mrs. Kapur's stray dogs' shelter last night? Just tied up the poor fellow outside in the middle of the night. I was going to see him . . . want to come?'

His eyes lit up. 'You like dogs?'

'Yup.'

'My mom doesn't let me keep one.'

'Nor do my parents. Come on.'

Dogs apart, there were other things they liked about each other, which made them a great team for mischief together. Sudha really was spunky, and if annoyed, would stick her jaw out and let loose the most colourful language to have ever left the lips of such a small girl, usually leaving her enemy red-faced and shocked.

'Where did you learn such words?' Lalit asked, admiringly.

'In the car when mom's driving,' Sudha grinned. 'She gets so worked up that she doesn't know what she's saying!' She made a face. 'Only, when I say the same thing, I get my ears twisted.'

'I'll bet you do!'

He had met her mom several times, and was a little scared of the thin, jumpy lady, who somehow reminded him of a canoe bouncing in whitewater. Her hair was always 'like a squirrel's nest', as Sudha put it, and she had flashing black eyes and a sharp way of talking. She was not to be messed with, he could see that, and so was exemplarily polite in her presence (which made Sudha giggle helplessly), always eagerly pulling out a chair for her and things like that, while she thanked him, her mouth curling up just a little amusedly. His mother, by comparison, was like a big, steady ship on a calm sea—though she could be very direct and terse when she had to be, and Sudha adored her.

Sudha could match him, trick for trick. She could climb a tree like a monkey, which made their raids on fruit trees a very successful operation indeed. In turn, she liked the reckless way he would invite trouble—he'd be ready for a fight no matter how big and how many the enemy were. At the Rescue Centre, where they loved to play with the puppies and dogs, he swaggered around, commanding them to 'sit' and 'stay' and 'down, boy!' while the animals paid him little heed and did their own thing, and then he would just get down and let them gambol over him and lick his face. 'Haha, the Amazing Conquest of Rambo the Dude by Little Balls of Fur,' Sudha would snigger. Truth was that she would really do anything for him, though of course she would never admit it to his face.

'Surprise? What surprise?' the children chorused now, looking around the shelter questioningly. There were puppies and dogs everywhere, in baby pens, roaming around, sleeping on the charpoy, barking, snuffling and wagging their tails. Some just sat quietly on old newspapers, their eyes sad and lustrous.

'Ramu found someone trying to drown these

little things in the pond in the park . . .' Mrs. Kapur said tiredly. She pointed to a cardboard carton on the floor.

'What?' Sudha stood stock still. 'Who was it? I'll kill them!'

'Oh, my dear, the fellow just ran away when Ramu challenged him.'

'Did he get a look at the villain? Lalit asked, frowning.

Sudha had already dipped into the box and was now cuddling two puppies in her arms. 'Lalit, pick up the other two,' she ordered, and automatically he did as he was told. Then he held one squirming black-and-tan pup at arm's length, quite professionally (he thought), and frowned.

'Auntie, he looks like a German Shepherd,' he said.

'We'll only know when he grows up, dear. I think he's probably a mixed breed. You know they're not worth any money, which is probably why someone was trying to get rid of them.'

Sudha looked up, her face red, and said a bad word that cannot be repeated here.

They played with the pups for about half an hour, and helped Mrs. Kapur with feeding and bathing some of the dogs, and cleaning their pens, as they always did, and then made their way home.

'How can people do such a thing? Really, if I were

Prime Minister, I'd have them shot!' Sudha tossed her head angrily.

'I'd burn them in oil!'

'I'd dunk them in acid!'

'I'd tie them to a cannonball and blast them!'

'Dip them in a tank full of great white sharks and piranhas!'

'You can't. The piranhas would eat the sharks.'

'No, the sharks would eat the piranhas!'

'No, the piranhas would!'

'The sharks would!'

'Piranhas!'

'Sharks!'

They stood by the kerb at the pedestrian crossing, hand in hand; their colony was just across the road. Lalit always told himself, rather loftily, that he only ever held her hand here to help her cross. 'She's flighty and scatterbrained; god knows what she might do—dash across suddenly!' he told himself. He had once told Sudha's mother, 'Don't worry, Auntie, I know, she's just a girl, and I'm older, too—I'll help her cross safely,' and Sudha had pinched him hard for the remark, and made a ferocious face.

Her mom had smiled sardonically and said, 'Thank you—that's so good to know!' But he was more careful while crossing than she was; often she would just drag him across, saying 'come on, slowpoke, that guy's miles away!'

'Hey, look!' he exclaimed suddenly, staring up the road. On their side, just a little distance away, was parked a beautiful silver-blue Porsche 911, squatting powerfully on its haunches, glittering in the sun. Wheee, he whistled between his teeth. 'Wait a sec,' he told Sudha. 'I want to take a closer look at it!'

She screwed up her face. 'Oh god, Rambo has seen a fancy car. Now Rambo will be mooning over it for hours.'

'Just look at it!'

'Okay, you look at it, I'll see you at home,' she said, suddenly jerking free and stepping out into the road. She waited for an autorickshaw to pass and then skipped ahead.

There was a terrible screech of brakes and a metallic *whang*!

And then a scream tore through the air.

Lalit stood transfixed with horror as he saw Sudha fly up, and then land and roll over and over and over. The bike that had hit her, shooting out suddenly from behind the autorickshaw and speeding down, stopped; the biker looked back and then fled. Lalit goggled, and saw his friend lying crumpled, a dark stain spreading around her on the road. And then the ground rushed up to meet him . . .

'Is she . . . dead?' he asked his mother, ashen-faced that evening.

His mother sat by his bed and shook her head. 'No, but she's hurt her head quite badly. She's unconscious. Her school bag saved her.'

'It was my fault,' he said dully. 'I let her let go of my hand. I got distracted by a Porsche . . .'

He saw his mother's face tighten; she did not say anything. Sudha's parents had been very upset and had squarely blamed him for the accident, and told her that in no uncertain terms. Her mom had shrilled like a banshee: 'He should have been more careful! I must have been mad to allow her to come home with him! What was I thinking?'

'He wants to visit her,' Lalit's mom had said quietly.

Sudha's mom's eyes had blazed and grown hard. 'Sure! Let him. Let him see what he's done to my baby!'

With steely courage and downcast eyes he went to see her at the hospital—fortunately, just next door—the following day. He didn't dare look at her wild-haired mother as she sat by the bedside, just fixed his gaze on his friend. Her whole head was wrapped in bandage like a turban, her eyes were closed and there was a livid bruise on her cheek. He hardly stayed for three minutes and left, swallowing great lumps.

But next day, there was good news. Sudha had regained consciousness and had been looking around her room, even if without interest.

'She'll be all right, won't she?' Lalit asked his mother anxiously.

'I hope so. She has a head injury, you can never tell.' His mother was not a person who hid things.

Lalit's mom was right: Sudha was conscious, but had awoken a completely different person: a very sad, depressed little girl, as if she was on the other side of a thick glass wall. She never smiled and her eyes were dull. In a few days, she was moved to a ward with three other children. Lalit visited her again. Her bandage had been removed and there was just a dressing in its place on her forehead above her left eye.

'Hi there!' he whispered anxiously. 'Are you feeling better?' But he was petrified. There was a blank, glazed look in her eyes; it was as if she did not recognize anyone or anything. It was like her eyes were dead, he thought.

'Sudha, it is . . . Lalit . . .' he tried, mock gruffly.

No reply.

'Remember those pups that someone had tried to drown? They're very naughty. They're driving Mrs. Kapur crazy!'

She stared at him and for just a second he thought he saw something flicker . . .

He had to do it. It was his only hope.

He stopped by the Animal Rescue Centre.

'Mrs. Kapur, can I borrow those pups for a while?' Mrs. Kapur, who had been feeling very sorry for him ever since the accident, smiled. 'You can keep them, if your mother permits,' she said. 'How's Sudha?'

'Not too good,' he admitted, his voice dropping. 'She doesn't seem to know me.'

'Maybe it'll do you good to play with them in the evening,' Mrs. Kapur said comfortingly.

'Thank you Mrs. Kapur. I'll pick them up at about five.' Then he went off to the park, and sneakily plucked a huge bunch of roses and dahlias and petunias, and dumped them unceremoniously into a large canvas bag.

Visiting hours were between 5 p.m. and 7 p.m. and, usually, Sudha's mother sat with visitors outside the ward, once they had seen the little girl. Her ward was on the first floor. Carrying a huge basket of somewhat bedraggled flowers, Lalit walked embarrassedly into the hospital, glancing about furtively. The huge security guard eyed him suspiciously and twirled his moustache, but his eyes softened when he saw the flowers. There was no sign of Sudha's mom outside the ward. Lalit knocked and entered the dim ward. He walked up to Sudha's bed and quickly drew the curtain around it.

'Hey, Sudha . . . see what I got you!' he said, proffering the basket of flowers. She opened her eyes and looked dully at the blooms.

'Idiot, not those—as if I would ever bring you flowers!' He shook his head in mock exasperation and rolled his eyes. 'Look inside!'

She raised herself on her elbow and peered into the basket. Four wriggly, squirming pups looked up at her and tried climbing out of the basket. One squealed.

'Shush, you silly thing!' Lalit hissed, taking the fellow out. 'Here,' he said, 'hold it.'

She took the pup gently from him and began stroking it. He stared, and then recklessly, took out another. 'Here's another.'

She smiled slowly and it was as if a small glowing light had suddenly been switched on in her eyes.

'Two for you and two for me!' He would have shouted had it not been a hospital.

Then of course, one of the pups jumped off the bed and scuttled off as quickly as she could.

'Oh shoot! Hang on to the others, I'll try to catch her!'

He drew back the curtain and looked around. The

child in the bed opposite was staring at the puppy and pointing, a smile lighting up his face. The children in the other two beds seemed asleep, though their visitors were staring at the pup in astonishment.

'Lalit!' Sudha squealed suddenly, 'the others have got away too! Catch them!'

Oh double-shoot, he was dead meat; there were now four pups running around the ward, in different directions. Sudha was sitting up in her bed squealing and giggling fit to bust, and the other kid was clapping his hands; even the visitors of the sleeping children had started smiling. A nurse burst in and looked around, just as one of the pups squatted and made a puddle.

'*Arre, ghoos*! Bandicoots!' she screamed and fled, bumping straight into the doctor and Sudha's mom who were just outside the door...

Half an hour later, Lalit sat quietly between his mother and Sudha's mom as Sudha's doctor and the Head of Administration looked at them sternly across the table. The expression on Sudha's mother's face was interesting. The stern, grim lines had gone, and she looked uncertainly at Lalit and his mom, tears brimming in her eyes.

'Well, madam,' the administrator said, sternly, 'normally I would have had to take strict action. Pets are most certainly not allowed in this hospital.'

'I'm sorry, doctor . . .' Lalit's mother said, giving Lalit a look that boded ill.

The doctor raised his hand. 'It's most unhygienic and undesirable. But in the light of the outcome, we shall let it pass. I examined the little girl. She's perfectly normal and cheerful now—she just needs to rest for a while and she'll be fine. She can go home tomorrow. I have to admit, it was the pups that did the trick.'

A few days later, Lalit visited Sudha at home and bumped into her mother.

'Er . . . hello, Auntie,' he said a little uncertainly.

She smiled at him. 'Come here,' she said, leading him into the drawing room. 'Sit down. I have something to say to you . . .'

'Is Sudha all . . .?'

'She's fine; in fact, I caught her trying to climb out of her window.' She put her hand on his cheek. 'Um . . . Lalit, I owe you an apology. Sudha told me what happened that day . . .'

'What . . .'

'There was no Porsche, was there? You made that up to protect her. She says she saw a pup trying to cross the road and snatched her hand away from yours, and ran across to it without looking.' ■

MRS. NARASIMHAN SENDS AN E-MAIL

ANU KUMAR

Every Friday evening, Raji would wait for Mrs. Narasimhan at the cybercafé. He would see her from a distance, her small purse in hand, lost in thought, sometimes fiddling with her hearing-aid, or sometimes peering through her glasses, hoping to catch a glimpse of him as he sat at his usual place.

Friday was the day Raji went to the post office, a 10-minute bus ride away, to get stamps and envelopes for Mrs. Narasimhan. She was getting old and the buses were now always more crowded than ever, and so Raji had offered to get them for her on Fridays. That day he had classes only in the afternoon. Besides, on Fridays, he ran errands for Ahmed Chacha as well, getting cartons of A-4 and A-3 sized paper for the photocopier in the shop and toner as well. He deposited bills that were due, picked up stationery, and the post office where he picked up stamps, inland letters and envelopes for Mrs. Narasimhan was on his way. He returned well in time for his classes, and in the evenings helped out at Ahmed Chacha's shop. It was an arrangement that suited everyone very well.

Raji worked in the cybercafé and also operated the photocopying machine. He had become very skilful at retrieving papers that sometimes got stuck deep in the machine (a skill that made him indispensable), and had learnt how to take copies in various sizes as well. Ahmed Chacha found Raji's help invaluable. For Raji, it gave him some extra pocket money.

Theirs was a small town by the sea, and the cybercafé was only a year old. Ahmed Chacha had got a few computers on a bank loan, and he worried incessantly if the net connection was too slow, for that irritated his customers more than anything else. The photocopier, he kept out of sentiment. Besides, as he explained to Raji, 'It's how I started and I can't do away with it. People will always have documents they want to copy. Applications, admission forms, certificates . . . nearly every piece of paper you own needs a copy sometime or the other.' And he laughed his great hearty laughter as if he had just cracked a joke.

The cybercafé brought in new younger customers and a regular bunch of tourists—even though the beach was a well-kept secret from the travel agents—and Ahmed Chacha was glad to have Raji around. The newfangled stuff, even if it brought him money, sometimes confused him. He was happier managing his booth, and happiest when talking to his old customers, like Mrs. Narasimhan.

On Fridays, an hour or so after Raji turned up at the shop, Mrs. Narasimhan appeared too. She always looked excited, for she enjoyed this chance it gave her to talk to Ahmed Chacha and Raji, and to say hello to other familiar faces who happened to be at the cybercafé then. She happily collected her envelopes, inland letters and stamps, and thanked Raji effusively, and over and over again, telling him he was such a nice and helpful boy always. This was her way, but it embarrassed Raji terribly. And Ahmed Chacha grinned on seeing him so discomfited. 'It makes her happy,' he said, 'all that you do for her.'

'I know, Chacha,' replied Raji, grinning self-consciously, 'I like doing it for her. And she doesn't have to thank me every week.'

Raji's own parents lived in their village miles out of the town and Raji wrote to them regularly. Though increasingly he preferred calling them, for as he admitted to Ahmed Chacha sheepishly, it was quicker and saved time.

Mrs. Narasimhan, on the other hand, wrote a

lot of letters—to her son Anand—Major Anand Narasimhan—far away at a border post in the desert, and to her grandchildren who were at boarding school in the hills. Sometimes she sent them photographs too. A phone call really didn't help for she was hard of hearing. Besides, the phone lines in faraway places were never good.

She loved to write letters, but you could tell she was happiest the days when she received one. She would turn up at the cybercafé, her eyes twinkling behind her thick spectacles, her lips spread in a wide grin as she greeted Ahmed Chacha and Raji in turn. Sometimes she would tell Ahmed Chacha and Raji about the letters, and read out parts to them. Ahmed Chacha had known Anand since he was a kid in the neighbourhood and always asked after him.

'Anand says he's fine and that I am not to worry. They have reduced troops this year and the governments are holding talks, so perhaps for a change, the border is likely to be quiet.'

Another day, Mrs. Narasimhan told them something else Anand had written:

'A young boy had crossed the border by mistake. He was looking for his runaway goat. No one knew when it had come over but we kept warning him as he climbed the rocks towards the border. Then of course we had to keep him for a few days, since he had broken the law. But all's well that ends well. We returned him to his parents yesterday.'

'Oh good,' said Ahmed Chacha. 'Imagine how miserable the child must have felt without his parents.'

'And in a strange land,' added Raji.

Mrs. Narasimhan would also tell them how hot the deserts got in the mornings and how considerably cooler the nights were. She spoke of the sandstorms, of the illegal infiltrators and the smugglers too.

In this way, Mrs. Narasimhan kept in touch with her son, in a far-away army camp on the desert border. Even Mrs. Narasimhan didn't really know where exactly, for he moved every week from one army post to another, returning on Fridays to the base camp. 'Don't show me the map, *beta*,' she would say, when Raji offered to show her his school atlas once, 'it will only make the place seem farther away than it is.'

Sometimes, she received letters from her grandchildren too. Sonali and Rohan were in a boarding school in Nainital and they would write and tell her all about the new exciting things they had done, the treks they had gone on in the mountains nearby, their painting classes, their exams and their teachers. Raji got to look at their photographs too, and invariably said, 'How tall they have grown. And so thin. They must be studying very hard indeed.'

And lastly she would go on to tell them how much her son and her grandchildren enjoyed her letters, and the photographs she sent as well. For Mrs. Narasimhan was an enthusiastic photographer though not an expert one. 'No, all those fancy digital ones are not my thing,' she said,' I use my old Agfa and it's served me well too. All the pictures of the fishermen bringing in the catch in the evening, the boats, the birds, the sea . . . my son and grandchildren really enjoy them. They live in the desert, and the hills, and miss the sea.'

On other days, that were not Fridays, Raji knew that Mrs. Narasimhan would be taking pictures or thinking up all that she would write to her son about.

'It a good change for her,' Ahmed Chacha explained to other customers who asked him why Mrs. Narasimhan spent such a long time in his cybercafé. 'And then it makes every mother happy if you ask her about her children.'

Raji liked the routine they had established. He liked to listen to her stories and felt he almost knew her family. He dreamed too of joining the army one day. There were times of course when he dreamed of being something very different, of climbing mountains or tramping through deep forests, like Mrs. Narasimhan's grandchildren.

When it rained heavily that first day in July, no one was bothered. It was a month like that, when the rains descended on their little town, and on a day out of the ordinary, it would rain exceptionally hard and everything would be thrown out of gear. Roads and lanes would get flooded, buses would stop plying after a while, there would be power-cuts in some places, there would be thin attendance in offices and customers would keep away from the flooded drains in front of shops.

This time the rain persisted stubbornly, for days and days. Sometimes, it would slow down to a drizzle but pick up in the next hour or so. And when this continued to happen for five days, Raji was unable to go to the post office and hated it because he couldn't bear to see Mrs. Narasimhan upset. Her expression said it all that Friday evening as she made her way to the cybercafé, wading through puddles, stepping across overflowing drains. A frown became etched on her face and wouldn't go away. Her voice, for all her efforts, trembled and the drops that fell off her umbrella could well be her own tears of disappointment.

It was that which made Raji blurt out, 'Why don't you learn how to use the computer, Auntieji? Then you wouldn't have to worry about all this . . .'

She didn't reply, but something made Raji persist.

'Am serious, Auntieji, it's easier than operating your camera . . .'

She looked at him and then laughed, an old lady's embarrassed laugh. 'Learning the computer? At my age?'

'There is no age, really,' explained Raji earnestly, 'and it makes life so easy. Your son or your grandchildren will receive your e-mail the second you write it. And then you will be able to send photos, your own photo, anything at all via e-mail.'

To him, these matters were so very obvious, but Mrs. Narasimhan looked at him as if he had made the most wondrous revelations that she would ever have the chance to hear. She gulped and he went on, 'You can try it.' Then because Ahmed Chacha was looking indulgently on, he went on, boldly, 'Besides, Ahmed Chacha is always looking for customers for his cybercafé. The photocopier doesn't make much for him.'

Later, Ahmed Chacha would swat him playfully on the head and say he had a rogue's head for business, but Mrs. Narasimhan didn't need more persuasion, and so her computer lessons began only a few days later.

'You are sure it won't . . .' she asked fearfully, her eyes big as saucers behind her moon-sized spectacles, the moment Raji pressed a button and the computer blinked to life.

'What . . . explode? No,' said Raji, trying to keep from smiling, 'it will just blink, make funny noises, ask questions like what's your password, but otherwise it's quite a meek, obedient machine.'

She ran her fingers gingerly over the keyboard. 'I used to work on a typewriter once, when I worked for a local newspaper. Do you think a computer would be the same?'

'Oh yes,' said Ahmed Chacha, piping in from his corner, 'except that a computer runs on electricity, and is a bit more complex and advanced; otherwise, it is much like a typewriter.'

Raji rolled his eyes at that blasphemous statement.

'You know,' began Mrs Narasimhan hesitantly, 'Anand did once encourage me to learn how to use one.' Her face clouded over, 'To tell you the truth, I can tell sometimes that my letters haven't reached him. One time, I could tell. He tried so hard not to upset me, but I knew he hadn't got my latest letter, in which I had told him of how the pigeons had made a nest over the skylight, and how their feathers had made a lovely mess all over my bedroom. I had also told him how the *bai*, Sunanda, hadn't been coming as her father's unwell. But all he did was ask me if Sunanda had been doing her work properly. So obviously he hadn't got my letter, in which I had told him about Sunanda's father and what a hypochondriac he is.'

'Oh, *tai*,' said Ahmed Chacha, turning the table fan towards her because even when it rained heavily in their town, it remained humid and a fan helped soothe tempers, 'it happens all the time. The post office people take their time to deliver to these remote areas. And also, they are government employees. You know how they are . . . they work only when they feel like. I am sure you will enjoy your computer lessons . . . and Raji's a patient teacher. Aren't you, Raji?' Ahmed Chacha's eyes twinkled behind his spectacles as he looked at the young would-be teacher and his much older student.

'You need to create an e-mail account for yourself,' explained Raji to her and it was easy because she could follow his hands as he spoke.

'Your e-mail account is like your letterbox,' he thought she would understand if he spoke in such allusions, 'and then you should have a password that only you know. It will be like a key that you keep with yourself.'

'I am sure I will forget my password,' complained Mrs. Narasimhan good-naturedly. 'How do you expect me to remember so many things at my age?'

'It has to be something that comes to you easily, and no, don't tell me,' Raji warned her, laughing, when Mrs. Narasimhan made to offer him several possible passwords.

In the beginning, of course, things took time and so Raji sent out e-mails on her behalf. She would speak very slowly and think things over too much, but Mrs. Narasimhan liked to follow Raji's hands as they skipped over the keyboard. She laughed at how quickly the words took shape on the screen. She liked following the dancing cursor as Raji pointed it here and there with every command she wanted to give. She always read the word 'send' aloud when the e-mail was all done. But she looked happiest when Raji downloaded her e-mail and she saw the e-mails she had received. Sometimes there would be one—for Anand was always regular in writing to her once a week. Her grandchildren wrote too, but they had access to e-mail only on weekends, and sometimes they had exams or went on school trips.

It did indeed surprise her that an e-mail was faster than any other piece of communication.

'You mean it will reach him the instant you press "send"?' she had asked once and then again.

'Yes,' said Raji, grinning. 'This very second. Zoom! it goes through space, from your outbox to his inbox.'

Still it did take Mrs. Narasimhan some weeks to get over her fear of the computer, and to get the hang of e-mail itself. Raji tried to make it easier when he showed her how he operated his own e-mail. He had several e-mail accounts—'for all my many activities,' he explained modestly, and then he was on several networking sites.

'They know all about you, Auntieji,' he said, showing her his Facebook page one day.

There it was, his Facebook status update that said: 'Teaching a mom to use the computer so she can reach out to her son at a desert border post.'

He read out to her some of the comments that followed from his friends. By now though Mrs. Narasimhan had learnt to read words off the computer screen with ease—no longer did its brightness make her blink—and she had learnt the keys to scroll down pages.

That must be the best thing you've ever done.

This sure is a faster way than just writing letters.

Nothing like receiving a letter, though. There is something sweet about seeing a loved one's handwriting.

Mrs. Narasimhan nodded as she read that and her eyes turned misty in the way they usually did.

'Yes, that's true,' she said. 'Even though Anand's bad handwriting is always difficult to read . . . like ants crawling all over the page. And Rohan, his son, takes after him, but he's already a whiz at the computer.'

They moved on to reading the next Facebook comment.

That's sweet of you, Raji. I remember how you taught me how to use an Excel worksheet.

'Is this a girlfriend of yours, this Susan?' teased Mrs. Narasimhan.

'No, no,' said Raji, and he blushed, 'she's just someone I helped.'

But the very next comment made him blush more.

That's right, Raji, you are always very helpful .

Mrs. Narasimhan laughed, 'I am sure I am going to make a comment like this one day too. And then you will say I am one of your oldest admirers.'

'Or the grandmother he's never known,' piped in Ahmed Chacha, for he knew Raji had lost his grandparents long ago when floods had struck their village.

There was an abrupt silence before Mrs. Narasimhan changed the subject. 'I think I owe you a treat for this. How about a nice piping dosa dinner for you one weekend?'

'That would be nice,' said Raji, and his voice sounded gruff with embarrassment again.

A week or so later, Mrs. Narasimhan composed her first e-mail. She had long lost touch with the typewriter so she moved her fingers awkwardly over the keyboard. She used the index finger of either hand and her speed was slow, and reminded Raji of two grasshoppers leaping terribly off-step. 'You can type in any language, you know that?' said Raji, as he watched her type.

Dear Beta Anand,

How are you? This is what I have asked you always as I will, even in this—the first e-mail I am actually sending you on my own. Raji here says this will reach you faster than a letter and I find that hard to believe. Still my thoughts are always with you, and thoughts don't need to run, anyway.

I hope it is not too hot there. I hope you are taking care and not taking any unnecessary risks.

Raji's the nice boy who has helped me with all this, and he's wonderful—his full name is Rajit Mishra, though he prefers to be called Raji.

Since this is my first e-mail, I will keep it short. But write soon, if possible.

Take care, that is the most important thing.

Yours ever affectionately,

Ma

'Are you sure it's okay?' she asked him nervously when she was done.

'Yes, of course it is. And you don't need to show me the whole e-mail . . .'

'Yes, yes, I know that,' she said, very impatient now, 'shall I send it then?'

Yes, and at a click the message flashed across her screen that her e-mail had been 'sent' and her delight was unfeigned. 'You mean that's really gone!'

Mrs. Narasimhan lost all fear of the computer after that. Within a week, she was operating her e-mail on her own, spending an hour at least in the cybercafé, laughing delightedly as she read softly to herself an e-mail she had received, from her son, his children or someone from her extended family who were scattered all over the world. When she received photographs, she would call Raji and even Ahmed Chacha if they happened to be around, and happily point out her children, her grandchildren, even though by now they could mark them out on their own.

Mrs. Narasimhan, however, didn't really give up her old habits. She still sent out letters in thick envelopes, gummed over with lovely stamps in the exact denomination.

It was a month or so later, that someone from the post office appeared with a carton-sized parcel. He was new and unfamiliar with most addresses, and so he stopped at the shop everyone did when they had to ask for directions: Ahmed Chacha's.

'A parcel for Mrs. K. Narasimhan,' he read out haltingly.

Ahmed Chacha pointed out the house to him, a small second-floor flat that faced the road, with its small balcony choc-a-bloc with flowerpots and the unruly bougainvillea.

'We must ask what this is about,' said Ahmed Chacha, watching the postman make his way down the road.

They didn't have long to wait. Mrs. Narasimhan turned up at seven, like she did every day now to spend an hour at the computer, and she carried lovingly in her hands a lovely handcrafted wooden boat. 'This is what Anand made for me, for my birthday. He was always good with his hands, turning out amazing things from wood chippings. And see, he remembered my birthday. I thought he had forgotten.'

'Well, well,' said Ahmed Chacha, 'this calls for a real celebration—Raji, here, go and get some samosas. And see, *tai*, you were right. There are some things an e-mail just can't do, like sending wonderful birthday presents to mothers.' ■

NINA'S MOTHER

PARO ANAND

'I wish she'd smarten herself up a bit,' sighed Nina crossly as she looked in disgust at the retreating figure of her mother. Her wispy, now-graying hair escaped the cheap rubber bands she insisted on using. The hem of her salwar had started to fray and her whole body sort of sagged down into itself as though carrying the burden of countless troubles.

'What burden does she have to carry, considering that she's home all day?' Nina wondered, her thoughts inevitably straying to Prashant Gujral's mother, with her trendily short hair, skirts and Italian leather boots. She was a hot-shot executive in a big five-star hotel and made innumerable trips abroad, bringing back iPod nanos and the best deos for Prashant.

'Here, Nanhi, I've made your favorite matar-paneer for you,' her mother smiled down at her. But Nina was so cross, she only scowled and thought of Prashant who would probably be eating spaghetti bolognaise or something exciting like that.

'Of all the mothers in the world, why did I have to be lumped with this one?'

She wished her mother would go to work or something, instead of frittering her life away in the house. After all, she was educated. Of course, she didn't have any particular talents, but surely she could at least be a secretary or telephone operator or something.

'I hope I never become like her,' shuddered Nina, sighing miserably.

She washed and changed and picked up her books. 'Bye, Ma, I'm going for my tuition class,' she shouted.

'Bye, Nanhi, do well,' her mother called back from the kitchen over the intolerable hissing of the pressure cooker. Her mother seemed to be in the kitchen all day long, 'and all she can come up with is matar-paneer and she doesn't even know it's not my favourite anymore,' muttered Nina meanly, as she slammed the door shut behind her.

Tuition class was cancelled. Mr. Basu, their teacher, had viral fever.

'Prashant, want to come over to my house?'

'I'd like to, Nina, but I can't. You see, my mother's

coming back from Bangkok this afternoon. I'll try and catch the driver before he leaves for the airport. Thanks, anyway . . .'

'What's she bringing for you this time?'

'I asked for the latest Nikon digital camera, it's too hot . . . see you around . . .' and he was gone.

'Bye . . .' Nina sighed morosely. 'A hot-shot camera for a hot-shot son from a hot-shot mum!' She grinned at her own feeble joke as she made her way back home. She was annoyed to find the door locked. Her mother had said she'd be going to the market in an hour, and here, she was gone already. Anyway, it was just as well, really. Right now, Nina didn't want any of her mother's fussing. Luckily, she had a key to let herself into the house. As she pushed the front door open, she heard a voice singing:

It is the evening of the day,
I sit and watch the children play
Smiling faces I can see
But not for me
I sit and watch as tears go by . . .

Her mother's bedroom was shut. The singing came out of there. Nina tried the door, but it was locked. She wondered who could be singing. The voice was rich and heavy, like honey.

It is the evening of the day
I sit and watch the children play
Doing things I used to do
They think are new
I sit and watch as tears go by . . .

Smooth as silk, the haunting voice and words rippled through the closed door to Nina. She stood with her ear pressed against it until the song had ended. Then, softly, she called out.

'Ma . . .?'

'Oh, Nanhi, you're back already?'

The minute the door opened, Nina walked in and looked around.

'Why, what is it? What are you looking for?'

'A music system, radio . . . I don't know . . .'

'W-what?'

'That song, where was it coming from?'

'What song?'

'Just now, the one I heard, something about tears and children, or something.'

Oh!'

Mother and daughter stood looking at each other in surprise.

'Well?'

'Well . . . I . . . it . . . that is to say . . . it's a song by the Rolling Stones.'

'And who was singing it?'

'Oh, they sang it themselves.'

'Come on, Ma, you know that's not what I mean. Who was singing it just now?'

'Now? What, right now? Why, I was, of course, who else is there?' And her mother laughed and turned away, as if embarrassed by the admission.

'But, but I didn't know you could sing . . .'

'Ha! "Could" would be about right. I could sing, it's true and I used to, in college. Played a bit of guitar too, as a matter of fact!'

'Wow! Why didn't you ever tell me that before?'

'Well . . . I guess because you never asked . . . before . . .'

Nina caught a glimpse of the hurt in her eyes and voice.

'But Ma, it was b-e-a-u-t-i-f-u-l! Why did you stop singing?'

'Oh, Nanhi, where would I have sung my Joan Baez and Bob Dylan songs? It's different when you're in college, but afterwards . . . it didn't seem appropriate somehow . . .'

'Surely you didn't have to stop completely? So completely that even your own daughter wouldn't know what a wonderful singer you were—are!'

'You know, Nanhi, I still love to sing. But when I was growing up, these things were considered a little, well, unladylike, improper—definitely not appropriate in a woman, a wife, a mother. You know, singing all these Western love songs and songs of rebellion. It used to upset a lot of people; even if I was singing unconsciously, without thinking. And the only way I could stop doing that was if I stopped completely. Your father and I lived in a small town, in a big family . . .'

'Don't you miss it? Don't you want to sing again? Don't you regret stopping?'

'Well, yes and no. I miss it, but I don't regret having given it up. I've gained other, more important things. And there's no point trying to recapture things once they've gone.'

'It's just singing, so what's gone? Certainly your voice hasn't.'

'No, Nanhi, those times have gone, for me, for us of that generation. We were all up in arms, rebelling, sometimes not even quite sure what we were rebelling against! We had so much fun. We'd have all-India competitions. We'd travel all over the country by train, in the third-class compartments, taking up whole coaches of university students all together. And we'd sing and dance all night long. Once, I was in a toilet and some others from another college were standing just outside and one of them said, "Now that Purnima and all are here, there's no chance of our winning." And the other one said, "Well, we could try and come second, at least!" It was such a thrill to be up on stage with everyone was clapping because they remembered you and your music from other competitions. And they'd all be stomping and clapping to the beat of your song. We always won—and the prizes and the standing ovations, you felt like you owned the world!'

Nina's mother's eyes were shining and her face was flushed with the memory of the exciting, heady times gone by. Nina looked at her in wonder, she'd never seen her mother like this—it was like getting to know a whole new person.

'So you don't sing at all now, Ma?'

'Now, sometimes, when I'm all alone in the house, I sing to myself, for myself. It makes me feel good, worth something. There are times when I feel so utterly worthless, good for nothing. Nanhi, I hope you never become like me. I hope that you will make something more of your life than I have. I want you to look back on your life and say, "I'm proud of me."'

Nina looked into her mother's face and saw in it an expression which she had never cared to notice before. She was spellbound by this change in her mother and watched as she spoke on, as if in a reverie.

'But I don't know . . . I think, all in all, it's been

worth it to me. Looking at you growing up—that means more than anything else in all the world, more important than any songs I could ever have sung, or things I could have done . . .'

'Oh Ma . . .' Nina sat at her mother's feet and put her hands into her mother's roughened ones. There was so much she wanted to say. To apologize, to show that she was sorry, that she would try and understand now. But the words stuck in her throat, not knowing which form to take. She was silent for a while, until the rush of emotions had subsided a bit. And then she said, 'Ma, sing another song, please, just for me?'

Her mother smiled and put an arm around her daughter's shoulders. 'All right, well, this is a song I sing for you sometimes, Nanhi, all for you; it's also by the Rollling Stones and it's called "Ruby Tuesday" . . .'

She would never say where she came from
Yesterday don't matter if it's gone
While the sun is bright, or in the darkest night
No one knows, she comes and goes
Goodbye, Ruby Tuesday
Who could hang a name on you
When you change with every new day
Still I'm gonna miss you . . .

Nina kept her head on her mother's shoulder.

Don't question why she needs to be so free
She'll tell you it's the only way to be
She just can't be chained
To a life where nothing's gained
And nothing's lost
At such a cost . . .

The voice filled the room and she was swept away on its gliding, glistening notes.

There's no time to lose, I heard her say
Cast your dreams before they slip away
Dying all the time
Lose your dreams and you will lose your mind
Ain't life unkind
So goodbye, Ruby Tuesday
Who could hang a name on you
When you change with every new day
Still I'm gonna miss you . . .

They sat quietly, holding each other's hands, holding onto the silence after the song.

And Nina thought, 'Of all the mothers in the world, I'm glad I got this one.' ■

MY LIFE IN PICTURES

DEEPA AGARWAL

The moment Vandita entered my room, I knew it had not been a good idea to invite her home. Because her eyes zoomed straight in on the collage behind my bed. The collage that was actually my life in pictures. And I wasn't particularly keen to reveal my whole life to her.

I wanted to impress Vandita—whom we all secretly thought of as the queen of the classroom. This was something that had always puzzled me, because there was no particular reason why she should be the most admired girl in VII B. She was neither good at studies or games, in dramatics or debate. She was not even a great dancer and could barely carry a tune. And yet whenever anyone mentioned Vandita, it was in a tone of hushed awe. Girls would cluster around her with silly grins on their faces the moment she appeared and say 'Hi, Vandita!' as if they were greeting a celebrity. She would respond with a faint Mona Lisa smile, without stopping to talk to anyone, and would make her way to her desk with an odd, rather grown-up expression as if we were too kiddish or rowdy for her. Instead of turning us off, it baffled us and made us all the more eager to be friends with her. But this proved easier said than done. Because while Vandita was nice enough, she wouldn't let anyone get too close to her.

Till the day she asked me to help her out with her maths.

I was so completely bowled over that for a minute that I couldn't say anything at all.

Finally, I was able to stammer, 'Y-yes, of course! P-please come over tomorrow afternoon.'

'Thanks so much,' she had said, in her soft voice, sounding as formal as ever.

And now she was here in person, right inside my room—gazing at the collage that was the embarrassment of my life!

'Who made this?' she asked.

I stared at her. Her face was flushed, her brown eyes gleamed. I'd never seen her so excited. I squinted hard at her to try and guess if she were making fun of it.

'My mom,' I replied, sagging with silent despair. Yeah, my trigger-happy Mom who thinks it's a matter of life and death to record each and every moment of our existence.

I cringed as Vandita's large eyes ran over the pictures—me as a ridiculously obese baby, perched inside a bathtub—completely naked. Me, waving a spoon with disgusting gobs of food smeared all over my face. Me, with my mouth wide open, howling like a lunatic. Me, as a toddler with my dress lifted up to my waist, displaying my panties without a care in the world. And then I had to suppress a scream—me on the potty! How could Mom have done that? Was it that important to record my very first civilized pee? Why hadn't it ever occurred to me to tear off that horrendous photo? Oh, why had I agreed to help Vandita with her maths? And why had she asked me? From feeling like the most privileged girl in class, I had sunk to being the most shamefaced.

The truth was, this collage was one of the reasons I avoided asking anyone home, other than my closest friends Bhavya and Riddha. Even though they rarely spared the opportunity to scream with laughter whenever they happened to look up at it. I could take it from them—after all, we had all grown up together and if they laughed too much I could shut them up by reminding them of the million embarrassing moments I had witnessed in their lives. But Vandita!

Oh my god, now she had her eyes fixed on that awful picture—the one of the folk dance for the school annual function! The gaudy Haryanvi outfit, rings of kajal around my eyes—making me look like an owl, one hip stuck out and an arm raised in a stupidly coy pose. Gawd, this was one moment when I would have given anything to own an invisibility cloak.

'Uh . . . would you like a juice or something?' Had she noticed that my voice was almost tearful? 'Th-then we can get down to the . . . the problems . . .'

'Oh, thanks, that would be great,' she replied in that soft, tinkling voice that reminded me of the sound of a dancer's ghunghroos. Only, the ghunghroos seemed to be much louder than I'd ever heard them.

I hurried to the kitchen and opened the fridge. I hadn't told my mother that a friend was coming over. I was too terrified that she might burst into the room to click the two of us engrossed in our studies—probably with the most ghastly expressions on our faces. Even though she'd made a pact with me—not to click any photographs except on special occasions like birthdays and festivals, and these too had to be approved before being printed and made into collages or preserved in albums for people to snigger at. In exchange I had agreed to let the collage remain on my bedroom wall.

'Can't you understand, sweetie,' Mom had said, 'how important all these moments are for me? When I look at them I think of you as an adorable little baby . . .'

'Then why don't you keep them in your room?' I yelled.

Dad had cleared his throat. 'No room,' he said, rolling his eyes.

'And then, Amanya,' Mom had continued in an almost tearful voice, 'whenever I enter your room, all those memories come flooding back.'

'Mom . . . don't you like me the way I am now?' I had glared at her. Then, 'All right, all right!' when I saw the dangerous look on her face.

All the same, I was not too sure if my mother would keep her side of the bargain. She was far too addicted to her camera. So I was always careful. But as they say—man proposes and God disposes. So while I proposed to carry two glasses of apple juice neatly arranged in a tray, along with a bowl of chips and a few generous slices of my mom's chocolate cake, to my room, without anyone knowing, God was making other plans. Now about my mom's chocolate cake—it is something that almost makes up for her camera addiction—it's the yummiest thing that ever went into your mouth. Sometimes I have a sneaky feeling that Bhavya and Riddha have remained my dearest friends since KG because of this wonderful cake.

Luckily, Mom had baked just the day before and if there was something that could erase the embarrassing impression those crazy photos must have made—it was the cake. I was smiling to myself as I entered my room, congratulating myself on this particular stroke of luck, when what did I hear but my Mom's voice at its highest, most enthusiastic pitch.

'Isn't that absolutely adorable? She was such a good baby. Unlike her brother, she took to the potty right away. Never ever did her business on the floor. We didn't believe in disposable diapers. At least I didn't. So bad for the environment!'

I almost dropped the tray. I wanted to scream and pull my hair. But I controlled myself somehow, reminded myself that I was almost twelve—quite grown-up. Next year I would be a teenager. I should try and act maturely, even though my mother couldn't.

Then Mom saw me. 'Amanya,' she said, 'you never told me a friend was coming over.'

'I forgot, Mom, ' I mumbled. Then I saw the camera in her hand. I put down the tray and took a deep breath. I looked sternly at my mother and shook my head. She looked down at the camera and bit her lip. I could guess at the struggle going on inside her. She looked pleadingly at me, but I shook my head again, even though, somewhere, I felt guilty about it. Mom's mouth drooped, her shoulders sagged and she nodded, then shrugged.

'Well, have fun, you two!' she said.

I sighed with relief. She was turning away when Vandita spoke in her tinkling, bell-like voice. 'Oh, Auntie, please . . . could you take a picture of us together?'

My mouth fell open. Mom looked at me confused. Vandita flung us a puzzled look. I clenched my teeth and said,' Yeah, Mom, why don't you?'

'All right,' she said expressionlessly.

She took several pictures in, of course, several poses. Vandita and me seated at my desk, frowning over mathematical problems. Vandita and me laughing at an imaginary joke, with our arms linked, looking as if we were lifelong friends. Vandita and me saying 'cheese' with all our might, just beneath the collage . . .

At that moment I got a brainwave. Now I had a good excuse to tear up the collage. Mom had not kept her side of the bargain. I knew she'd make the excuse that it was Vandita who had asked, but I would stand firm. After all, she could have said something like, the camera battery was not charged, or it just wasn't working, or anything at all. She had exploited the situation and I would not forgive her for that.

Our study session went off fine. I went to see Vandita off to the gate and as she was leaving she said, 'Please, please e-mail all those photos to me. I'm dying to show them to my parents. Your Mom is such a great photographer!'

'Of course,' I said. 'I'll ask her to transfer them to the computer right away. See you tomorrow in school!'

I would have to find a way to slip this in while having a showdown with Mom. In the meantime, I ran back to my room. My hands had been itching to tear up that horrible collage for so long that they could hardly wait.

But I found the wall bare. The collage was gone! Mom had been smart enough to remove it before I went on the rampage. At first I felt cheated—then relieved—then oddly ashamed. The wall looked so empty!

'Have you gone crazy?' I scolded myself, as I dragged my feet to my parents' bedroom. You hated that thing and now that it's gone you're missing it? But I had to tell Mom about sending the photos to Vandita.

She was lying down on her bed and half sat up when she heard me enter. Her face went red.

'Well . . . she asked me to take the pictures . . . okay . . . I violated our agreement—so—I've removed it!' she said in a rush.

I felt even more ashamed. She looked so worried and guilty. I had forced my mother to make explanations to me. It felt awful. Of course, Vandita had asked her. How could she have refused? And why was I making such a fuss over something so silly as a few baby pictures?

'It's fine, Mom,' I said, hanging my head. 'You couldn't help it. But . . . I would never have destroyed the collage. How could I? Isn't it my life in pictures? My whole life till now?'

Mom laughed and laughed and gave me the tightest hug ever. Then she said, 'Wait a second, I'll put it on automatic and click this moment.'

I groaned inwardly. But of course, I agreed. Well, after all how could my Mom change? And then it struck me—did I want her to? After all, this is what made her unique!

There's a little more to tell. Vandita printed out the photographs and brought them to class. And no points for guessing who the most admired girl in the class was, after this! ■

PEECHU

MARGARET BHATTY

'Peechu pagal! Peechu mad! Peechu pagal! Peechu mad!'

The class closed in on Peechu, stamping their feet as they chanted. He raised his arm and hid his broad face in the crook of his elbow. Lower and lower he bent until he was doubled over on the floor near his desk. That way he couldn't see his tormentors. He didn't understand what they said, but he knew they were being unkind.

'Children! Stop that and return to your places!' the teacher ordered. They scampered back to their seats. Standing over Peechu, she said severely, 'Now, tell me what you did with the crayon I gave you?' Her voice was harsh. It made him curl even tighter.

'He ate it, Miss,' someone said. 'I saw him.'

'Don't be silly. Only mad people eat crayons—' she countered. The remark was a mistake. The children again began to chant: 'Peechu pagal! Peechu mad!'

'Silence!' she cried.

'But he *is* mad, Miss,' a voice said. 'My mummy says he's mad!'

Bending over Peechu, the teacher tried to uncurl him. But he was heavy for his eight years and she couldn't lift him. She rummaged in his pockets for the crayon. 'Stones!' she exclaimed, emptying his new school shorts and making his precious pebbles clatter on the floor. From her tone Peechu could tell she didn't approve of them.

'*Neah! Neah! Neah!*' he bleated. Without looking up, he groped and tried to collect them into a small heap.

'Get up at once and tell me what you did with that crayon!' she said.

'Miss, he ate it,' someone said. 'If you look at his mouth, it's all red.'

The teacher shook Peechu roughly by the shoulder, hauled at his arms and then left him, curled over on the floor. His mother found him there when she came to take him home in the afternoon. But before she lifted him and led him away, she had a long talk with the teacher. Peechu recognized the bitterness in her voice.

That was Peechu's first—and last—day at school. He'd been so happy getting into his new clothes, like everyone else. But he knew somehow that he'd spoilt it all. His white shirt had a large pink patch where he'd dribbled after eating the crayon. The school didn't want him back.

Though his schooldays were over, Peechu kept wearing his uniform. He returned to chasing crows and sparrows on the rubbish heap behind the tumble-down building where his mother had a small room under the staircase. He returned to looking for pebbles in the sand heaps on the building site across the street.

When he found a really smooth one, he held it in his hand and kept passing his fingers over it. Or he rubbed it slowly against his face. And when his mother came down the street, back from work, he ran to her and held it against her face. 'Huh? Huh?' he asked, looking for her approval.

Pebbles were special things for Peechu. Her shabby handbag was heavy with pebbles he had given her. Some were tokens of his love. Some were simply to say he felt good inside. Some said sorry, he'd made her cry. Most of them were because he'd made her cry in despair, sorrow, anger and defeat.

Peechu's mother worked as a data-entry operator

in the Corporation office, close enough for her to hurry home in the middle of the day, open her room, feed him, clean him up if need be, and make him go to the bathroom before locking up again until five. Peechu's father had abandoned them when he was three. She never had time to teach Peechu anything. And when she stopped to talk with neighbours coming down the stairs, her voice was bitter. 'Look at my *kismet*,' she wailed. 'Abandoned! And with only an idiot son to look after me in my old age!'

Peechu was happiest digging in the sand pile for pebbles. He didn't look up when the children passed on their way to school. 'Peechu pagal!' they called. 'C'mon with us! Teacher will give you nice crayons to eat!'

He hid himself in the crook of his arm, bent over till his nose touched the sand. They filled his hair with it, put handfuls down the back of his shirt and into his shorts. He stayed curled up tight until they went away.

Trucks came during the night and dumped more sand on the building lot. Lying beside his mother, Peechu saw their headlights rake the wall opposite. There, on planks for shelves, among clothes and other things, were rows of smooth round pebbles. In the morning, the neighbourhood children swarmed over the sand heaps and slid down their sides until the chowkidar shouted and chased them off. Only after they'd all disappeared did Peechu shamble out, his large head held sideways, his mouth half open. Sitting on the heap, he clawed at the sand and brought out the river stones hidden inside. Coloured, flecked, layered and lined, worn smooth by the flow of the river.

So absorbed was he that he didn't see the woman until she was very close. 'Who has dumped all this sand on the road?' she asked. He looked up and gaped. Instead of legs, she had wheels!

'Help me get this thing to move,' she said, struggling with her wheelchair, which had sunk deep into the sand. He didn't respond, though he kept staring, his mouth open in a smile, his tongue thick between his teeth.

'He's not right in his head,' Peechu heard his mother say. She had crossed the street when she saw the white-haired old woman in difficulty. She pushed the chair and got it clear.

The wheeled woman gazed at the two—Peechu, overgrown, broad-faced and foolish, and his mother thin, worn and shabbily dressed. 'Does he go to school?' she asked gently.

'Which school will take him? I put him in the Tiny Tots nursery here, and the teacher told me he needs to be sent to a special school. How can I afford a special school? And what's she being paid for if she can't teach him anything?'

Still complaining, she hauled Peechu to his feet and led him off. He shambled along, crab-walking, so that he could still stare at the wheeled chair in which the woman sat. Wheels! Wheels for legs!

Every morning after that the wheeled woman came down the street to find Peechu waiting on the sand heap. He pretended she wasn't there until she asked to see his pebbles. Then he held them against her face. 'Huh? Huh?' he asked, moving them gently on the back of her hand. She nodded and smiled, and he knew she liked what she felt. She liked his stones!

Laughing widely, he pushed his face closer and closer, his thick tongue trying to form words. 'Stop that!' his mother's voice said, and he drew back quickly. She had come to take him inside.

'Can't he talk at all?' the wheeled woman asked.

'Who has time to talk to an idiot child?' she asked bitterly. 'But he knows how to get his way when he wants anything. He bites, kicks and scratches——'

She held out a hand to show the teeth marks left when she'd tried to make him take off his new school uniform. 'Stones!' she said with disgust. 'All he cares for is stones. He spends all day looking for them. Then he strokes them. He even wants them in our bed at night.'

Peechu was familiar with the bitterness in her voice. But suddenly he didn't care. The wheeled woman hadn't shown any disgust, the way everybody did. She liked his pebbles too.

Shuffling off across the street to their room, he came back, breathing hard, his eyes shining. 'Hah!' he cried and tossed a large pebble into her lap. It was a perfect one, the best he'd ever found, egg-shaped, slate blue and utterly smooth.

She exclaimed at its beauty, turning it on her palm. He pushed at her hands roughly. 'He means you to keep it,' his mother said.

'It is very beautiful,' the woman said.

'He has never given his wonderful stones to anybody else before,' his mother said. 'That means he likes you.'

Peechu's education began with him being allowed to push the wheelchair. He was big for his age and even strong, but clumsy. Sometimes, he almost tipped it into the gutter.

The wheeled woman lived at the end of the street, in half a house. She had wondrous coloured things growing in her garden. 'Smell this,' she said, holding one under Peechu's nose. He thought she meant him to eat it, so he did.

'No! No!' she cried. 'Flowers aren't for eating!' But she wasn't angry.

Inside her house she had yellow birds in a cage, coloured fish in a bowl of water and countless priceless crystal animals along shelves. He loved the feel of them between his fingers. He began to learn their names.

He learnt five good words the first month—names for the wheeled woman, the two women who looked after her, his mother, and the man who looked after the garden. He began to polish his collection of pebbles. He changed his clothes and bathed. He didn't do all this so easily. He refused. He threatened to bite and scratch. He cried '*Neah! Neah!*' to the two women.

The wheeled woman gave him his pebble back. 'I don't want it if you don't listen,' she said without anger. Peechu was aghast. She had rejected his gift! He raised his arm and hid himself in the crook of his elbow. Doubling over onto the floor, he sobbed himself to sleep until his mother came to fetch him. She talked a long time with the wheeled woman and the two others who helped her.

'If he is too much trouble, I will stop him from coming here,' she said.

'He can be taught,' the wheeled woman said. 'Look, he made this pebble shine, polishing it with emery paper.' Her voice was warm. Peechu was sorry for the way he had behaved. He again pushed his favourite pebble into her hands before he left. Once again she said, 'Thank you. I am happy to have it.'

And he felt happy to have won her back.

The egg-shaped stone was placed on a special stand on the table at which Peechu worked. It had taught him to listen. Next it taught him control.

The second time his gift was rejected was when he started learning to make curves and lines on his slate. He grew so tense trying to make his chalk do them right that he exploded with the effort. Smashing his slate on the floor, he ground the chalk under his heel, bawled with fury and defeat, and deliberately swept some of her priceless crystal animals off the shelf. He stood and gazed at her for a moment. She said nothing. Then, reaching across the table, she held out his pebble. He had lost her approval again and it upset him very much.

'*Neah! Neah! Neah!*' he blubbered and went down on his knees to pick up the remains of his slate.

At the end of six months he had learnt to say twenty words. But inside his head he had stored up many more—which he couldn't get off his heavy tongue, however hard he tried.

Now when he pushed the wheelchair along in the street the children gazed at him with open envy.

They dared not shout 'Peechu pagal'—not when he was out with the wheeled woman.

The very first word Peechu learnt to write so filled him with astonishment that he ran all the way home to show his mother.

'Look!' he said and wrote it in large letters on the front door with pink chalk. MaMaMaMaMaMa . . .

He worked the same magic on the walls, the cupboard, the floor and outside the building. The children gathered around curiously. 'MaMaMaMaMaMaMa . . .' they read, until the writing ran off the wall and he had to continue it onto the tarred road.

'Read—' he said, almost distinctly.

'Mama!' they read. 'Peechu pagal has written his mother's name!'

'Peechu pagal! Peechu mad! Peechu pagal! Peechu mad!' they chanted, without any unkindness, and as they sang they stamped their feet. Peechu joined in.

He had done it! He could read and write—just like them.

It had taken him a whole year, but he had done it. Peechu had done it! ■

FURRY LOVE

RADHIKA MEGANATHAN

There was a gleaming crimson Mercedes-Benz parked outside my house. I whistled. Who could it be? One of my sister Anitha's rich friends? I entered my home, and a booming voice pierced through my skull.

'Manish *paiyya*, how are you? It's been so long!'

A big hand descended on my cheeks, pinching it so hard that I wished I was a dog. I could then snap my head away and bite the hand.

'Do you remember who I am? Huh, Manushkush? Do you?' I winced at the endearment. With every question mark, her fingers pulled the skin off my cheek. It was like a torture scene in a spy movie. I yelled, 'Yes, Auntie, I remember you! I remember you! You were Amma's best friend in college!'

'Good, good,' shrilled the terrible voice, 'wonderful to know that you haven't forgotten your auntie. You were only this high when I saw you last . . . how you have grown!'

Mercifully, I was released. I could see my sister, laughing silently. Rubbing my reddened cheek, I glared at my torturer. She was a giant of a woman next to whom my dainty mother looked like a mosquito. Fortunately, Malu Aunty missed my glare and was busy leaving our house, babbling to Amma about vacations, Lufthansa and . . . Johnny?

My blood turned to ice. So much for wishing to be a dog. Had she brought her demon dog with her? *Here?*

Amma came back, and before I could ask her anything, she said: 'Malu is visiting going to New York to visit her sister. She wants us to take care of Johnny for a couple of months,' she said, looking for a reaction from me. She got it, certainly.

'Nooo . . .!' I screamed. If possible, I would have fallen on the floor and howled, but I was tired after the cricket match, so I settled for a vocal temper tantrum. 'No, No, NO! He will NOT stay in my house!'

'Beta, Malu was desperate. She could not leave him at the vet's because he doesn't get along with the other dogs. I will make sure he doesn't hurt you, okay?'

Noooooo! I kept screaming, hands on my ears. 'I hate dogs, you know I do! I can't believe you agreed to have him here. He has to go! Or I will!'

Anitha got up from the couch, looking disgusted. 'Manish, stop being a drama queen. How can you be scared of a little dog like that? Gosh, are you a girl or what?' she said, rolling her eyes.

That was rich, coming from her! Her permanent hairstyle is a crew-cut, and her permanent attire is jeans and a T-shirt. I threw my badminton racket at her, which she caught deftly and threw back at me.

'So, where is *he*?' I asked, not letting my fear show in my voice.

'Amma has chained him to the desk in her study,' replied Anitha, and left.

Amma's private study. It used to be Dad's; it still had all his stuff there. Even we were not allowed there without permission. I tiptoed across the corridor. Opening the study door, I peered inside. A pair of malevolent canine eyes turned on me. It was Johnny, the Demon Dog, the Pomeranian from Hell. He recognized me in a millisecond, and lunged. I shut the door, and ran back to my room.

It was at Usha Mami's engagement that I came across the Demon Dog. The engagement ceremony was on the ground floor, and the place was full of smoke from the *havan,* and giggling friends of the bride. I was roaming around the upper floor, riffling through the various almirahs.

Well, what can I say? I am attracted to unlocked cupboards filled with curios and knick-knacks. I like to take them out and admire them. Not that I am a thief. I am NOT. It's the only way to pass time when you are stranded in an old house, where everybody is smelling of flowers and giving you slurpy kisses and piercing you with their pointy diamonds.

So there I was, an innocent nine-year old boy, harmlessly looking at a misshapen toy kite from an almirah, when a barking hurricane descended upon me. I remember thinking, King Kong! Or may be I thought, T-Rex! I screamed so loudly that the pandit downstairs stopped chanting his mantras.

What happened next is the usual stuff. The womenfolk thought it was a thief, the menfolk came barging upstairs with sticks in their hands, and there I was, going round and round the room, up the sofa and down the chair, with the yapping, snapping Demon Dog stuck to my trouser leg. I was hastily saved, and quickly interrogated. Luckily, I had told my sister that I was going upstairs to the bathroom. It was concluded that I had entered the wrong room and encountered the mad dog.

But hey ho! The dog was apparently a darling pet, who was meek as a lamb. Everybody was astonished at its sudden murderous intent. Only I knew what was going in his mind.

The dog never forgot seeing me with my hand inside his owner's almirah. Apparently, the first Supreme Law of Canines must be, 'Once a thief, always a thief'. And now, he was in my house, in my Amma's study, looking at me with a malevolent grin.

I went to look for my mother. She was in the kitchen, preparing dinner (a revolting mix of doggie pelts and cooked chicken) for Johnny. She was humming. I left without talking to her.

The next few days were unbearable. The dog occupied Amma's time and attention 24/7. She worked as a teacher in my school (don't get me started on *that*) and hardly spoke to me there, because she didn't want others to think that she favoured me. I usually didn't see her till dinner, as she took special classes after school and came home quite late. But she made up for it by cooking us a great dinner (I love the crunchy dosas she makes) and we would watch our favourite TV shows while eating. After that, she would chat with us about our day and sometimes even join us in my pillow fights with Anitha.

But now when she came home, the first thing she did was prepare Johnny's food and take it to the study. She spent all her time there, grooming him and petting him; it was always Johnny this, Johnny that, until I wanted to make a furry cushion out of him

and sit on it. She didn't join us for dinner anymore, and didn't even notice when Anitha stole my dosas. She was either bathing or walking or kissing the darned dog. I got so fed up of the whole thing that the inevitable happened.

I put an end to it.

Two weeks after the Evil Dog took over my house, Amma brought Johnny out for a walk. She had started doing this every day when Anitha and I were having our dinner, claiming that the walk was good for her. Ha! As if I didn't know she was doing it for the dog? Seeing me on the living-room couch, he bared his teeth. I returned the compliment.

Suddenly, Johnny froze. He looked at the open door, at the landing, where the resident cat was washing its face. She locked eyes with Johnny, and paused for a millisecond before making a run for her life.

Jonny went crazy. Obeying the Second Supreme Law of Canines ('Thou shall chase felines at all times'), he struggled to pull himself away from Amma's hold. She tried to rein him in, but he shook free with a sudden strong jerk.

'Manish, close the door!' Amma yelled. I was sitting on the sofa, my hand just inches away from the door. All I needed to do was move my left arm and push it against the open door, and it would snap shut, before the dog could make it across our huge living room.

I didn't. I just sat there like a sack of potatoes. The dog, panting with excitement at a possible cat chase, managed to make it out of our house.

My mother stood with the empty leash in her hand, her mouth open in shock. She then ran out of the door, shouting Johnny's name, while I sat stupidly in the couch, my eyes glued to the rerun of *Dexter's Laboratory*.

Johnny had been missing for half a day. Not that I cared. I was happy that I could walk without fear in my own home.

Anitha came back after her sleepover night at her friend's, to find the house devoid of one dog, and occupied by two silent humans. I waited in my room, knowing she would come and start to yell at me.

My sister surprised me. No pillow throwing, no big-sister lectures. 'Why didn't you close the door, Manish?' she asked me softly.

'Because I don't want him here!' I yelled at her back. 'I shut the door because he is always with Amma. She never has time to take us anywhere, but she is walking him every night. She is always petting him, coochie-cooing him, cooking for the monster . . . she knows I can't stand him, but she chose him over me. She doesn't even know that I exist anymore!'

Anitha was silent for some time. Then she sat beside me, while I blinked furiously, trying to keep my tears at bay. Boys don't cry, right?

After a while, my sister spoke. 'Do you know that Johnny's mother used to be our dog?'

I stared at her. This was news to me.

'Yeah, it was when Dad was with us. Sheba was Dad's pet and he loved her very much. But you were so terrified of her, Amma gave her away to Malu Aunty.'

She rubbed her eyes. 'You know, Manish, after a point, you have to give instead of receiving all the time.'

I saw Amma sitting hunched in the kitchen, a plate of uneaten food before her. Johnny had now been missing for a whole day. She was probably thinking how to break the news to her best friend.

I spoke, before my courage ran out. 'Amma, I am sorry I let Johnny run away.' I whispered, in a small voice.

Amma sighed. 'I know you hated him, Manish. It is my mistake. I shouldn't have agreed to look after him. But he reminded me of your Dad . . . I thought . . .'

I muttered something under my breath, but it wasn't in any language I knew.

Amma didn't hear it. 'He's just a dog. Now he is lost, out in the city. I don't know what to tell Malu.'

'Please, Amma, I am really, really sorry . . . I will help you find him. I will design a poster in Photoshop and print it out. I can put it up on all the lamp-posts . . .'

She was not listening. She was looking at a point beyond me. I turned and saw Johnny at the doorway, panting. He looked tired but happy.

'Oh, Johnny,' cried Amma, running to him. He snuggled up to her, soaking up the attention. Then she said a surprising thing. 'I am going to board him in a kennel, Manish. I can tell Malu that you have developed an allergy to dog hair. She will not mind.'

I looked at my mother. I could see the worry lines on her forehead. She is always ready to leap onto an invisible sacrificial altar for us. I kicked myself mentally. What my sister had said was true. It was high time I did something for her, for a change.

'Don't worry about Johnny, Amma? I am not scared of him anymore,' I said, lying through my teeth. Maybe I wouldn't be, after a while. 'We can keep him here till Malu Aunty is back.'

Amma smiled at me. I took cautious baby steps towards them, and was stunned to see Johnny wagging his tail at me. 'One day out in the streets . . .' spoke an evil voice inside me.

Or maybe Johnny could actually feel my change of heart. Who can tell? But when I saw Amma smile, I swear that had I a tail, it would have been wagging twice as feverishly as Johnny's. ■

THE PRINCESS OF BEANS

SUBHADRA SEN GUPTA

Madhura's long fingers hovered thoughtfully over the baskets of flowers for a moment. Then she picked a jasmine and a marigold, swiftly wove them into the garland, and then picked a deep red rose, sniffing happily at its fragrance. Madhura was making a garland for her favourite god, Lord Vishnu. Every morning the first garland she made was always for Him.

She was sitting in her mother's flower shop, a small space with a thatched roof, piled with baskets of flowers and bowls of incense. Their shop was the busiest in the street because it was closest to the gate of the Vaikuntha Perumal Temple in the royal city of Kanchipuram. The tall, arched gateway led to the newest temple in the city that had been built recently by their king Nandi Varman. It led into a beautiful shrine where in the sanctum stood her favourite god—Lord Vaikuntha Perumal, that is Lord Vishnu in the form of the king of the universe—clad in golden garments, glittering with precious jewels and wearing a tall gold crown.

Her mother had taught her to always string the first garland of the day for the god. As she said often to Madhura, their livelihood depended on many pilgrims coming to worship at the temple. Madhura liked to think that the garlands she made were all laid at his feet. Every morning she and her mother came to the shop with baskets of brightly coloured flowers—red and pink roses, creamy white jasmines and orange marigolds, and bunches of green bel and banana leaves. They sat at the shop and threaded the flowers and leaves into fragrant garlands and pilgrims going into the temple bought baskets of garlands, rose petals, incense sticks and earthen lamps that they offered to the god.

The shouts of the palace guards made her look up, 'Here comes the princess,' thought Madhura, eagerly leaning forward to look, 'she is early today.'

As she watched, her eyes bright with interest, Princess Jayalakshmi got out of her palanquin and came walking slowly down the narrow lane. As always she was going to the temple for her morning puja. Madhura's hands lay still holding a half strung garland as she sat mesmerized, staring at the royal procession. The palace guards came first, carrying shiny spears and wearing tall turbans. Behind them the princess came strolling along, surrounded by her companions, who were followed by a row of maids carrying large silver platters filled with flowers, fruits and incense.

Madhura carefully studied what the princess wore that morning—a long skirt in green silk embroidered in gold, a short blouse and a golden veil, sheer as gossamer, floating around her shoulders. Madhura was nine and she guessed that the princess was twelve or thirteen.

'What a pretty necklace!' thought Madhura in wonder, staring at the princess' gold necklace—a row of tiny pendants shaped like mangoes set with red rubies. Then she took a closer look at Jayalakshmi's face and thought as she did every time she saw the princess, 'Why doesn't she ever smile?'

As Princess Jayalakshmi swept past, she did not notice the little girl in the flower shop who watched her with such wide-eyed admiration. Madhura would have been thrilled if the princess had smiled at her but she never even looked her way. Princesses were too important to notice poor garland girls.

'Amma,' Madhura turned to look at her mother.

'Why is the princess coming to the temple every day? She never did before.'

'She is to be married soon,' her mother replied as she sold a garland to a customer and then counted the coins. 'I heard that her mother, our Queen Rajyalakshmi wants her to do the puja for a month. She is praying to Lord Vaikuntha Perumal for a happy married life and many sons.'

'I wish she would come to our shop,' Madhura said dreamily. 'I'd weave a special garland for her made only of jasmines and red roses.'

Her mother laughed, 'Stop dreaming, child! She is Princess Jayalakshmi, daughter of King Nandi Varman, of the great Pallava dynasty. They have gardens in the palace and maids to string garlands. She would never come to our shop for flowers.'

'Why not? Aren't our garlands pretty?' Madhura frowned.

'It's not that. It is because we are poor,' her mother's eyes were gentle as she looked into her daughter's wide-eyed face. 'The rich and the powerful do not notice poor people like us. They just walk past like the princess does. They never see our faces, they never talk to us . . .'

'Why not?'

'I don't know. You'll have to ask a princess one day.'

'She wears such pretty clothes and jewellery,'

Madhura looked down at her simple blue cotton skirt, all faded after many washes, 'but have you noticed, Amma, she never smiles?'

'May be princesses are not supposed to smile,' her mother's quick laugh told Madhura that she was teasing. 'You'll have to ask her that too.'

Madhura tied a string of jasmines around her hair and said briskly, 'If I were a princess, I would smile all the time!'

Later, while her hands were busy stringing the garlands, her mind was busy with her thoughts: 'The princess is so lucky! She wears a new dress every day and even changes her jewellery. She has maids to do all her work and friends to play with. And she must eat such delicious meals—the best rice cooked in ghee, fresh fish from the sea and desserts like payasam filled with raisins.'

She thought of the small thatched hut in which they lived, with its hard earthen floor on which they slept on thin woven mats. 'In the palace she must have a big room, a soft bed and a pool to bathe in. She wouldn't have to walk to the river to bathe.'

That evening Madhura and her younger brother Sivaraman waited for their father to come back from work. He was a weaver and worked in one of the workshops that made silk saris for the royal household. Then as the family sat down to eat their simple dinner of rice, sambar and a beans-and-coconut dish, Madhura said suddenly, 'If I was a princess I would never eat beans.'

Her father gave her a startled look, 'Who's a princess?'

'Madhura has been watching the Princess Jayalakshmi every day,' her mother explained. 'I think she wants to be one too.'

'If you become a princess, then I'll be a prince!' her brother said with a wide grin. 'Prince Sivaraman!'

As the others began to laugh, Madhura said stubbornly, 'What's wrong with wanting to be a princess? I'm sure she leads the happiest life in the world!'

'Aren't you happy?' her mother asked curiously. 'I thought you were.'

'I would be Amma, if you were a queen!' Madhura explained patiently. Mothers never do understand, do they? 'The princess is so lucky she has Queen Rajyalakshmi as a mother! The queen buys her silks and jewels and she never walks in the heat and always travels in a palanquin. And she doesn't have to make . . .' Then she stopped, noticing a sudden flash of sadness in her Amma's eyes before she went back to eating.

'Ah!' said her father solemnly, 'so it is all your Amma's fault!'

'Umm . . . not really, Appa . . .' Madhura took a quick look at her mother's bent head and then had to admit, 'Amma can't really help it.'

'Then stop dreaming of being a princess,' her mother said firmly. 'What is so bad about your life? Why do want to be a princess?'

'If I was a princess then I wouldn't have to eat beans. That is why!' Madhura protested, holding up a handful of beans and coconut. 'I just, absolutely and totally, hate beans!'

'Aha!' her father nodded, 'Now I understand! It's all about *beans*!' He grinned at his wife and announced, 'Our princess Madhura hates beans! Remember that! No beans in this house!'

'What about me?' asked Sivaraman plaintively, 'I *like* beans, Appa!'

From then on, her father and Sivaraman began to call her the Princess of Beans and it made Madhura absolutely hopping mad. 'No one understands me,' she brooded, sitting gloomily in the flower shop, 'they just know how to tease and laugh. What is so wrong with wanting to be a princess?'

One morning, a few days later, as the princess was going past, Madhura turned to look at her mother and discovered that she was busy at the back of the shop. She crept out and followed the royal entourage into the temple. They entered an open courtyard and then walked through a pillared corridor that led to the main shrine, where the priests stood at the door to welcome the princess. They led her inside to the sanctum where the image of Lord Vaikuntha Perumal stood, surrounded by the golden glow of tall brass lamps and wreathed in incense smoke.

'Will she pray at all the three sanctums?' wondered Madhura because this was a very special temple. There were three sanctums, one on top of the other with three different images of Lord Vishnu. On the ground floor He was sitting on a throne like a king, on the first floor He was standing and blessing everybody and on the third, He was reclining as if at rest. Madhura liked the standing image the most; it had the kindest face.

A small crowd had gathered to watch and the royal guards pushed them back roughly and made them stand in the hallway. Madhura stood on her toes and managed to catch a glimpse of the princess standing before the god, holding a handful of flowers as the priest raised the many-flamed *arti* lamp and began to chant the mantras. Madhura leaned against the cool stone of a pillar and looked around happily. She liked temples, the smell of incense and flowers, the clang of bells and the raised voices singing mantras. There were images of Lord Vishnu everywhere, carved on the pillars and placed in niches of the walls.

'So when is the wedding?' a man spoke next to Madhura and she turned to see the two royal guards standing on the other side of the pillar.

'Next month. Our princess is going far, all the way to Thanjavur.' Madhura's ears perked up and she crept closer to listen.

'I hear the queen is not happy about the princess being married into the royal family of Thanjavur.'

'And neither is the princess.'

'But what can they do? The king decides and the queen and princess obey.'

'They say the Thanjavur prince is much older than our princess and already has two wives.'

'Poor little princess. I heard from a maid that she cries often and is also scared of going so far away.'

'But she will have to obey His Majesty.'

A thoughtful Madhura wandered back slowly to the shop. Later, when the princess went past on her way back to the palace, Madhura looked at her sad face and thought, 'Thanjavur is so far away! She may not come back to Kanchipuram for a long time.' Her heart thudded with sympathy. 'Imagine going so far all alone and then not seeing her Amma and Appa, for years and years . . .'

That evening Madhura was helping her mother cook dinner while her father and Sivaraman were lounging around watching them and cracking bad jokes. As she chopped a pumpkin she said, 'I went into the temple after the princess today . . .'

'Oh, that's where you went!' her mother turned to look at her. 'I was looking for you. Next time tell me before you leave.'

'What was the princess doing?' Sivaraman asked.

'I saw her do the puja and then I heard two palace guards talking. They said the princess will have to go to Thanjavur after her marriage.'

Her mother was busy cleaning a plate of rice, carefully picking out small stones and pieces of husk. She raised her head and widened her eyes in this very dramatic way, as if she was worried, 'Oh no! Now would you want to follow her and get married and live in Thanjavur too?'

'No, Amma, I won't.' Madhura said patiently. Why wouldn't adults ever let her finish what she was saying? 'I don't want to ever leave Kanchipuram.' Then she added with a small smile, 'Unless you come with me.'

Her mother gave her a thoughtful look, 'Do you think the queen will go with the princess?'

'I know she won't, but then wouldn't the princess miss her?'

'Of course she will. And that is why I'm going to marry you to a boy who lives right here in Kanchipuram. So I can see you whenever I want.'

'What if Appa wants to send me far away?' asked Madhura anxiously, remembering what the guard said about the queen having to obey the king.

Her Amma turned to glare at her Appa, 'Then I won't listen to him!'

Her father shrugged, 'I always obey your Amma. Didn't you know that? So I'll find you a boy in Kanchi and also make sure your mother-in-law never cooks beans.'

'Here we go again!' Madhura glared at him. 'Appa, can't you think of anything else except *beans*?'

'How can I?' his grin widened. 'As your father, I'm the King of Beans, remember? And your mother is the Queen . . .' and then he and Sivaraman laughed so much Madhura wanted to hit them. Instead, she put her head into her hands and pretended to weep, and that made them all laugh even more.

That night over dinner, her father had some exciting news. That day a royal minister had come into the weaver's workshop and bought up all the saris for the princess' wedding. So all the weavers were given a special bonus of a month's salary and next evening they were all going shopping.

'I want a red skirt,' said Madhura, very excited, 'with a gold border.'

'Can I buy some marbles?' asked Sivaraman.

'Do you think we have money to buy a new rice pot,' her mother wondered, 'a brass one?'

'Yes!' smiled her father. 'And we'll get new thatch for the roof and maybe build another room. I'm feeling rich today!'

'Then we'll also have dosais at the food shop,' her mother said happily, 'and I won't have to cook.'

'And a bowl of payasam too!' added Sivaraman with a hungry grin.

That night, lying on her mat, Madhura dreamed happily of red skirts and marbles, dosais and payasam, jasmines and roses . . . Then as she was about to fall asleep, she thought, 'So what if my mother's not a queen . . . it's not bad being the Princess of Beans.' ■

Author's note: *The beautiful Vaikuntha Perumal Temple still stands in Kanchipuram in Tamil Nadu. It was built over 1200 years ago by the Pallava king Nandi Varman II. It is one the oldest temples of India, where worship has continued unbroken since the eighth century.*

The Princess Jayalakshmi and Madhura, the flower girl are imaginary characters but I did buy a basket of flowers at the temple gate from a smiling little girl with big, dark, heavy-lashed eyes, and pink ribbons in her hair. She is my Madhura.

RUNAWAY!

JYOTI PANDE LAVAKARE

Dear Mom,

By the time you get this email, I will have run away from home. Don't worry—I am a big boy now. I'll prove it to you in a minute, by spelling out my entire plan to you. I've been working on it for more than a month now, right down to this email. In fact, the reason I left you email instead of the traditional note pinned to my pillow is because I know you open your email only after 11 a.m. when you are done with all the housework and your morning phone calls, so I'll get more lead time. See how clever I am? I can certainly take care of myself.

First, let me tell you my plan, so that you stop fretting, worrywart that you are, and then I'll tell you why I was forced to take this step, okay?

Here's my plan; I have booked an e-ticket for myself on the Lufthansa flight via Munich to San Francisco (the exact same flight Daddy always takes on his business trips six times a year, so I even knew the flight number!). I had to use his credit card to buy the ticket through his favourite site—Orbitz. I must say I was happy to find a really cheap ticket, even though I wasn't proud of myself for lying—I had to pretend to be Dad to buy it through his ID. (But you know how easy it is to be someone else on the Internet—I can be just about *anyone* I want.) I don't know if Dad is going to be impressed with me that I managed to do all this by myself—or just hopping mad, but either way, I just had to get out of here.

I'm not worried about the flight—we've done it so often as a family, and besides, I don't even have to change terminals at Munich. Okay, I am anxious, just a little, especially about the connection. I don't want to reach some other country by mistake, especially not one where they make slaves of small boys or make them camel jockeys, working 18 hours a day like they showed on the HBO programme we all watched together. Yes, I know I'm being silly, because my Geography is good enough for me to know that Munich is not exactly in the middle of a desert, but I must admit I am a little apprehensive (that was the longest word in last month's spell-sheet, btw, and I googled it—it means a little more than uneasy and a little less than scared. Yup, that's me all right.)

So although I'm not exactly afraid, I'll sure be glad to get home to California, I can tell you.

I've already sent Charlie an e-mail, asking him to come and pick me up at the airport. He won't tell on me, he's totally promised—and he isn't my best friend for nothing. In fact, it was his idea to tell his mom only on the day I'm supposed to arrive there and not before. He said he has soccer practice that evening, and he's going to say he has a stomach-ache so that he doesn't have to go. That way, they'll both be home around the time my flight arrives. And that is when he will tell her she needs to drive him to the airport. Charlie's mom will do anything for him (unlike certain moms we both know) and he's promised he'll make her bring him to the airport, even if has to hold his breath until he goes blue in the face—he says Anne can't hold out to that particular tantrum, and always gives in!

Of course, when I tried that tactic (remember last month when you refused to buy me the second nunchuk to the Wii, and insisted I should earn it with good behaviour?), you just stared at me in amazement, and then walked out of the room saying, 'I can't believe that someone whose teachers don't tire of telling me how brilliant he is and how precocious with an IQ of over 135, can behave in such a childish manner. Whenever it is you decide to breathe again, please let me know, so that we can resume our discussion.'

Discussion! It wasn't even a discussion, with you just telling me what I have to do. It is always telling telling telling. Doesn't a boy have any rights around here? Which brings me to why I'm running away in the first place. Did Dad and you ever even think of checking with us kids whether it would be okay with us to move from California to Delhi? Hello! Palo Alto was my home! I was born there, I began school there. It's where I want to live, not silly old Delhi where I can't even drink water straight from the tap without dying from cholera, where no one stops for us to cross the road, even at zebra crossings, and scary looking ladies with puffy orange hair and bloodstained teeth yell at you for stopping your car at a red light. At a red light! And that reminds me, I don't believe your pawn story. Pawn cannot make your teeth bright red, and anyway, why would anyone be eating chess pieces! Ha. Gotcha. You lied. Again. Like when you said we would enjoy India and begin to love it more than Palo Alto. Never. Over my DB.

Anyway, apart from it being stinky and dirty and hot and full of shouting and rude people here, I can't walk to school like I did back home—I have to spend 150 minutes of my life every day in a bus getting to and from school, ending up with no time to play. That is so not fair! Compare that with Palo Alto, where I got home with lots of the day to spare, only to go out and play, and Daddy came home every day while it was still bright outside, and we all went biking or running or played hoops right around the corner from where we lived. Here, I barely even get to see Dad on weekdays; I don't get to rollerblade or bike in the neighbourhood on my own, meet my school friends every evening, or do any of the other fun stuff I used to do. Even the weekends here are boring, except for my tennis lessons and tabla classes. And on top of all this, you won't even get us the hamster Dad promised us in India. Maya and I have been asking for a dog for years, which you and Dad cleverly negotiated down to a cat, then a rabbit, then a hamster and what did we finally end up with? A pair of goldfish—but at least we lived in Palo Alto then and not in this silly boogerhead place!

I wasn't exaggerating, Mom, when I told you you've ruined my life. Charlie says I'll probably need years of therapy to recover from this trauma, but he also said he'll ask Anne to begin work on me as soon as I reach Palo Alto—thank goodness my best friend's mom is a psychotherapist! At least, she's not going to say things like 'Oh but Adi, look around you, you have a better childhood than most,' when I grumble. You're always pointing to beggar children at the traffic lights,

Mom. But why must I always compare myself to them? What about all my friends in California who are doing all the things I was doing, snowboarding and racing bikes and having a great childhood without feeling guilty? Remember, the really cool thing we did in third grade last year? My class studied a village in Africa, we collected funds through a Read-a-thon to build a well and buy 50 goats for that village, and they sent us pictures of all those happy villagers who thanked us? I thought that was awesome! Instead of feeling sorry for people and guilty for having more, we found a solution, however small, and learned to share. If a class of 22 kids and our two teachers could do that, then . . . oh well.

So, when I get there, both Charlie and I are going to beg Anne and Peter to adopt me. Charlie's parents are really cool—you and Dad used to like them, I know, so I think you would approve. His dad is an Imagineer with Disney—how cool is that!—and they would be totally fine with what his mom calls 'blended' families. (Charlie said he is ready to give up his cat, KB Johnson, for me, if needed, and that will be one of his bargaining tools. Isn't that cool too?)

In fact, Charlie has an ace up his sleeve. A couple of months ago, he heard his parents discussing adopting a baby girl from China. We're going to tell them that this, our solution, is much better. Anyway, Charlie doesn't want a snotty-nosed, squalling baby—a girl at that!—in the house, and we both agree I will be a much better companion to him than that kid. Charlie and I are counting on his parents. His mom is really super-nice (and her almond fudge cookies are better than yours, sorry, Mom!) and Peter is really cool, though a little too nerdy. Sort of like Daddy. But overall, I think he'll make an awesome dad, kind of like Daddy, but with a little more time.

This is not about Daddy or you—I love you both, and even that domineering sister of mine and Bumble (bet you didn't know Maya has an imaginary dog—he's a cross between beagle and a pug, super-ugly and super-cute!)—but I really can't bear to be called names in school every day by dumb boys who think they are smart, but don't know the difference between football, rugby and soccer. They laugh at me because I can't speak Hindi fluently; they tease me about my accent, and the fact that I don't know their games! Tell me, Mom, if you heard your classmates chanting 'Go back home, US boy! Go, go go,' every single recess for a month like I did, wouldn't you feel like running away too? And you call this 'building character'? Oh, you are so wrong! Next you'll say it will build my immunity to more global bugs! Phooey.

I hope you and Daddy will accept that although

I will always be your son, I cannot and will not live in India and be forced to love it.

Your son forever (but not in India),

Adi

Dearest Adi,

Firstly, let me say how very glad I am that the taxi driver refused to take you to the airport and brought you right back. It is noon now, and you are still fast asleep in your room, your chin tucked into your stuffed bear's paws, looking more innocent and lovable than is legally allowed for a boy of your age! You can't imagine how I feel each time I re-enter your room to reassure myself that you really are safe and not on a strange airplane, flying alone to unknown destinations at the mercy of absolute (and possibly murderous) strangers.

Actually, none of that would have come to pass; I'm just playing out your fantasy. Even if you had managed to reach the airport and snuck past the security at the entry gates to the airline counter, they would have needed parental consent to allow you to travel unaccompanied, especially out of the country. At some point, some adult somewhere would have noticed a little boy with a big backpack, a green strolley and a hairy-beary stuffed toy (why did you decide to take Paws? I thought you were so over him!), and turned you in. I wasn't sure if that look on your face when your plan was foiled, was disappointment or utter relief, but I have to say, both Dad and I were very impressed with the way you'd worked out all the details of your elaborate plan! However, you heard Dad last night: if you ever do anything like this again, you will be in Big Trouble and your computer privileges will be taken away, not just for a month, like this time, but for the entire year. Possibly for the rest of your childhood (which will really make it even more awful than it currently is, so watch your step, young man.)

I decided to write you an e-mail because I can't wait for you to wake up, especially since I also estimate that that may take a while, given how exhausted you must be and how late you finally slept after all the brouhaha settled.

More importantly, there were things you said in your e-mail that caused Dad and me serious concern and I want to respond, calmly and objectively, without either losing my temper with you, or hugging you hysterically. Therefore, this e-mail. I'll try and go point by point.

But first, I want you to understand that Daddy is not being 'crool' when he—we, actually—decided to take away some privileges, which include no computer, no television and no phone calls to Charlie for a month, beginning tomorrow, Monday. We want you to use this time think about what you almost did and how it could have turned out for you—and us. This is called introspection, and we both want you to do a lot of that this entire month.

I realize that these past six months have been tough for you. Although you may not realize it, I have been watching you struggle with a suddenly-new environment, a new country and culture and friends, even new family, or at least bits of existing family that you weren't previously aware of. I have observed you dealing with huge changes in every aspect of your life and strange and mysterious (for you) local traditions and customs with courage and aplomb—and I have been proud of you. You have come to terms with your new life and adjusted very well.

Oh, yes, you have complained. Loudly and clearly. We heard you.

But I remember one little boy in Palo Alto who sulked for an entire day because his muscle sprain didn't allow him to go for the school winter ice-skating party, and so he refused to join Charlie and Blake for a movie, or do anything else instead, but just wallowed in self-pity. The same now not-so-little boy last month was happily trying to devise creative ways to pass a Saturday afternoon when he couldn't go for Varun's birthday party because he had a Delhi-belly. And why? Perhaps because, like us, you too have learnt a little to go with the flow, to become more accepting of changed circumstances and more tolerant of people around you.

'Yo mom, cut the lecture. If you're proud of me, just gimme back my computer time, okay, dude,' you'll say as you read this. I know you, better than you think I do. Oh, and by the way, Mr. Know-It-All, it isn't the chess pawns I was talking about, it is 'paan'—a very typical Indian thing people eat that stains their teeth red. It is basically a betel leaf (heart-shaped, big, shiny green leaf that you chew) with a bunch of edible pastes, *chuna* and *kattha*—the closest translation I can think of is white lime and catechu—but you can check Wikipedia if you want more information. When you have your computer privileges back, that is.

Regarding being adopted by Charlie's parents—you are right, I do like them, a lot, actually, but somehow I don't think it'll be so easy to get adopted by them, or anyone else, for that matter. Usually your biological parents have to be dead or willing to give you up, neither of which we are at present. Plus, your 'bossy' and 'domineering' older sister would be completely lost without you!

Adi, we all make choices in our lives, and Dad and I truly believe that our move to India will toughen you both. You would have preferred the American

School, but seriously!—one of the reasons Dad and I chose to bring you guys back to our country (and which we hope you will one day feel is your country too) wasn't to live in an expatriate bubble, replicating to the last Kellogg cornflake your US life, but live the Indian reality. Surely you could be 'Born in the USA,' but also be 'Made in India,' couldn't you?

When we lived in Palo Alto, we tried to integrate ourselves there—we celebrated Rosh Hashanah, Halloween, Chanukah, Christmas and Diwali with equal gusto, learnt western classical music and baseball—why can't we learn tabla and Odissi, kho-kho and *pitthu* here, as and when we get the chance. We'd want you experience (whether you enjoy or hate) a *laiyya patti* from a street-side cart over its highly processed and over-packaged cousin, the rice crispy.

Now before your eyes glaze over, here's some good news cloaked as bad news—and then some real good news. You're not getting a hamster. Did you know mommy hamsters actually eat their own babies? I don't think I could deal with that. But don't be disappointed—what Dad and I want to do to help you get through this tough time in your life is this: we're going to get you and Maya a dog of your very own! A real one, not like Maya's Bumble! You can choose whichever breed you want, as long as it won't grow to be taller than you (so no St. Bernard nor a

Great Dane!), but I promise that after your month of introspection is over, I will go with you to dog shelters so that we can get that dog for you. Of course, you will have to feed it, train it, clean it (including poop), bathe it and walk it. It may help to make your life seem less ruined.

With lots of mommy-hugs to the best and cleverest 9-going-on-100-year-old in the world,

Mom

P.S. I will also try and bake cookies as tasty as Anne's in future—I thought your favourite were brownies, never even knew you like almond fudge. Duh! And, oh. Dad has promised to come home early at least twice a week to play with his best buddy, Adi.

Dearest, darlingest Mom,

You rock!! A dog!!!! Woohooooo! I'm going to call him Musibat, to remind you of me . . . and to remind me . . . of India (as if I can forget!).

Hugs and kisses,
Adi

P.S. India isn't that bad, actually. Especially now that we will soon have an Indian-born puppy and become a blended family ourselves . . . ■

THE STAR MOTHER
An Indian Folktale

KANIKA SHARMA

A long, long time ago before even memory was created, something extraordinary happened. The three most beautiful girls in the universe were born to the Star Mother. The mother glowed with joy, while all around her, zillions of shooting stars danced and blazed with happiness.

The eldest daughter was the most beautiful; she had long lustrous golden hair, gem-like eyes and a radiant smile like her mother's. They called her Sun.

The middle one was one in a million, unlike anyone the galaxy had ever known or seen. Waiflike and soft, she was always difficult to catch, giving only a fleeting glimpse of herself now and then. But sometimes, she would be strong and stubborn and forceful, powerful enough to blow everything away. She was named Wind.

The youngest one was very different. She was pockmarked and dark, with silvery hair. Extremely shy, she hardly appeared in front of anyone except when it was dark. She was Moon.

The Star Mother was very fond of Sun and Wind, even though they would often be in trouble, and the Star Mother had to keep an eye out for things that would go haywire. As they grew older, the Sun, with her blaze, would set fire to things unknowingly, and the Wind would gush at such speed that something or the other always ended up broken. But they were extraordinary and the whole galaxy was in awe of them.

Moon was a mystery to all, including to her mother. She would glide gently everywhere, and when she appeared she evoked the same calmness in the most ferocious of creatures. Sun and the Wind would snigger at her kind and sweet ways.

One day two unexpected guests arrived at their home. They were standing against the light in the doorway and had the strangest silhouettes Sun, Wind and Moon had seen. The one on the left was zigzag in shape, and very tall and thin at the same time. The other was the exact opposite. It was shorter than the girls and was so rotund that the girls thought it was the zigzag's luggage. As the Star Mother had gone out, Sun being the eldest, tried to approach the doorway. Yet as Sun drew closer she heard a rumbling noise that seemed to be coming from somewhere inside the luggage.

This scared Sun, and she was more than ready to set the poor luggage on fire. Wind came, with a swish and a rustle, to help her sister blast the two visitors away. 'No, don't!' said Moon, with her usual mildness.

Behind them was the Star Mother. When the zigzag and the blob turned to greet their mother, Sun, Wind and Moon realized that the visitors were their relatives—Aunt Lightning, and the luggage—Uncle Thunder. They wondered at their Uncle Thunder—a stocky round man whose grin was as wide as he was tall! Even though he was funny, his roaring laughter startled them no end. His laughter, you see, was louder than the rumble of his stomach; it made them feel as if the roof over their head, and the ground beneath their feet were falling at the same time.

Aunt Lightning was always flying into a rage over everything. She flickered and flashed so sharply that it seemed that if one went any closer, one would be cut into two. Sun, Wind and Moon had never imagined that their mother, who was always happy and tolerant, could have a sister who had such a temper. Yet, the Star Mother was very fond of her cousin Lightning.

Their uncle and aunt stayed for a while and then invited the three sisters to have dinner with them, and their mother allowed them to go. She said she would wait for them until they returned and asked them to behave themselves.

Sun, Wind and Moon dressed themselves in their best clothes. Sun shone brightly, and Wind flounced alongside, while Moon glowed, lending her surroundings a white silvery light.

The moment they reached their Aunt Lightning's place, Sun, Wind and Moon looked around in awe and wonder. The whole place was covered in a swirling white mist that cleared when they stepped into it, and then spun around again. Uncle Thunder came to the doorway to greet them and suddenly the mist turned dark grey. By the time the supper guests went indoors, the mist became sparkly white again.

Their house had sheets of ice for a floor and beautiful droplets for walls and ceiling. Oddly enough, the house, rather than being cold, was cool and pleasant. Finally their Aunt Lightning appeared, for once with a flickering smile, making Sun, Wind and Moon sigh with relief.

A rainbow covered the ceiling. On the table, there were iced goodies off mountaintops, and cloud-soft spoonfuls that became the flavour you liked in your mouth. Oh, it was a supper to remember! Seeing all this, Sun and Wind ate more than their stomachs could take and still didn't feel satisfied. They were very greedy indeed and did not leave as much as a tiny morsel of food on the table. But Moon ate slowly, and kept half her heaped plate aside to be packed.

Finally it was time to go and the three sisters bade goodbye to their aunt and uncle, and started for home. On the way, Sun and Wind kept racing each other, while Moon followed them slowly, carrying the package of food in her hand.

By the time they reached home, it had grown very dark and Moon was glowing again. They found the Star Mother waiting for them.

'What did you bring me from the supper?' she asked.

Sun tossed her head of golden hair in disdain and indifference as she answered her mother.

'I had gone out for my own enjoyment and not for yours,' she retorted. 'Why should I have bothered to bring you anything?'

Wind, on the other hand, put forward a lame excuse, 'I followed what Sun was doing. The food was so delicious, Mother, that I completely forgot about you. Anyway, it's not as if you've never had it before—you have known Aunt and Uncle longer than we have, right?'

While such arguments were taking place, the Moon quietly opened the bag she was carrying and laid out a meal for her mother. The Star Mother's eyes welled up. She had spoilt and pampered Sun and Wind, who had not bothered about her, while only Moon had cared enough to think of her.

The Star Mother spoke first to the Sun. 'You were thoughtless and selfish, my daughter,' she said. 'You didn't even think of me when you were out enjoying yourself. As nothing comes of ungratefulness, it will be your extraordinariness that will haunt you the most. Hereafter, you shall no longer be beloved among people. Your rays will always be hot, and burn everything they touch. People will hide themselves from you, and run away from you.'

And that is why, to this day, the Sun often blazes and scorches.

Next, the mother spoke to the Wind. 'You, too, my daughter, have been greedy and foolish,' she said. 'You blindly followed your elder sister, without a thought for me or anyone else. You will forever run with the rays of your sister, withering and burning all that you two touch. Yet, if you turn to your sister Moon, and blow in her light, you will always be loved like her.'

And that is why, to this day, the Wind blowing in the heat is unpleasant, and so soothing in moonlight.

The Star Mother then embraced her kindest daughter, Moon.

'You remembered your mother, and were unselfish,' she said. 'For all time your light shall be cool and calming. Despite the so-called ugly marks on your face, people will call you beautiful. Your presence will make all the stars look brighter. Also, you will always guide to safety those who venture out in the dark.'

And that is why, to this day, the Moon is so cool, and bright and beautiful. ■

THE STORY OF MOTHER'S DAY

A 12-year-old girl, Anna, in West Virginia, US, was listening to her mother Ann Marie Jarvis, say a prayer at school, at the end of the lesson on 'Mothers of the Bible'. Ann Marie said: 'I hope that someone, sometime, will found a memorial mother's day commemorating her for the matchless service she renders to humanity in every field of life. She is entitled to it.'

Anna Jarvis never forgot these words.

She had always been a very affectionate daughter who lived with her family in West Virginia. She was the ninth of eleven children. Her family, headed by mother Ann Marie Jarvis and father Granville Jarvis moved to a town called Grafton when Anna was a year old. Anna went to school here, and then to Augusta

Female Academy in Staunton, Virginia, now called Mary Baldwin College. After college, she returned to teach in a school in Grafton.

Her mother was always an inspiration to Anna. Despite her large family, Anne Marie Jarvis regularly participated in church and community activities. Her major contribution was to help form Mother's Day Work Clubs in the local churches, to improve the poor health and sanitation conditions prevailing in those times in their neighbourhood, which caused children to fall sick and even die. The clubs were very successful. After the death of her husband in 1902, Ann Marie moved with her daughters, Anna and Lillie, to Philadelphia to live with her son, Claude. She died at the age of 72 on 9 May, 1905. On the day she was laid to rest, the bell of her hometown church in Grafton was tolled 72 times in her honour.

When her mother died, Anna recalled her words from long ago and vowed to make her mother's wish come true. In 1907, she began an aggressive campaign to establish a National Mother's Day in the US. Along with supporters, she began to request, ask and cajole powerful people, by writing them hundreds of letters, to declare an official holiday on a day honouring mothers. To celebrate Mother's Day, on her mother's second death anniversary, Anna began to send carnations, her mother's favourite flowers, to her local church, asking people to wear them to show their love and gratitude to their mothers. A white carnation was to be worn to honour deceased mothers, and a red one to honour a living mother. She spoke about it every chance she got. Slowly but surely, the idea caught on, and in 1910, West Virginia became the first state to recognize Mother's Day as a holiday. By 1911, it was celebrated in every state in the US. On 8 May 1914, President Woodrow Wilson signed a Joint Resolution, designating the second Sunday in May as Mother's Day in the US.

Long, long before that happened, the ancient Greeks observed a kind of Mother's Day: they celebrated a yearly spring festival, to honour Rhea, the mother of many gods and goddesses. The Romans too had a spring festival called Hilaria to honour Cybele, a mother goddess, around 250 BCE. In England, around the 17th century, Mothering Sunday was celebrated: poor children who were apprentices with rich people were, on this day, sent to visit their Mother Church (the Cathedral of their hometown) to honour Mother Mary during Lent, the 40-day period of fasting leading up to Easter. The children met their mothers after going to the church, and presented them flowers and special 'Mothering' cakes, and fasting rules were relaxed on that day. The date of this Sunday varied every year, as it was on the fourth Sunday of Lent.

Before Anna Jarvis went all out to found Mother's Day, Julia Ward Howe, a feisty writer, poet and reformist, had written a Mother's Day Proclamation in 1870 in Boston, US, in support of celebrating Mother's Day as an official holiday. The idea had caught the interest of some people—but it didn't turn into a holiday or countrywide celebration.

It was Anna Jarvis who finally made it happen, making her the founder of Mother's Day. She died at the age of 84, on 24 November 1948. She is buried beside her mother in Philadelphia, and the bell in the church in Grafton was rung 84 times in her honour. The Anna Jarvis Birthplace Museum is located four miles south of Grafton.

Anna Jarvis never became a mother herself, though. And she grew increasingly bitter about the fact that people didn't make an effort to show their mothers that they really cared—instead, on Mother's Day, they just sent a printed card and were done with it. She wrote: 'A printed card means nothing except that you are too lazy to write to the woman who has done more for you than anyone in the world. And candy! You take a box to Mother—and then eat most of it yourself. A pretty sentiment!'

So make every day Mother's Day—show your mom you care! ■

25 FUN THINGS TO DO WITH OR FOR MOM

1. ARTWORK KEYCHAIN

You know how your mom loves to keep everything you draw. She will love this keychain too.

You Need:

• a small colourful drawing • glue • cardboard • scissors • clear varnish • paintbrush • a very small metal ring • a key-ring

MAKE IT!

1. Paste your drawing on a piece of cardboard. When it's dry, cut around the drawing.
2. Apply two or three coats of clear varnish, letting each coat dry completely before the next coat.
3. Ask a grown-up to make a small hole at the top of

the drawing and push the small ring through it.

4. Now loop it into the key-ring.

2. ONE-ON-ONE

Make your mom feel really special by making a single-focus project on her. You can make it like a small magazine—and she will treasure it forever.

You Need:

- a scrapbook
- photographs of your mom
- pens/colours or use printouts

MAKE IT!

1. Start with something like a magazine or TV interview (either take notes or record it). Prepare a list of questions for your mother—starting from her childhood, and going on to school, college, career, marriage and so on. You can also add other sections, such as Favourites, Pet Hates, What Makes Her Laugh, and comments from your dad, relatives and her friends.
2. Then either write everything by hand, or use printouts, to make a scrapbook on your mom.
3. Make an attractive cover—and gift it to your mom.

3. FAB FLOWERPOT

You can make paper flowers for this easy-to-make flowerpot, or fill it with soil and plant seeds in it, for real flowers for your mom!

You Need:

• a Styrofoam cup • colourful buttons
• craft glue • acrylic paints • paintbrush
• scissors • green tissue paper

MAKE IT!

1. Paint the cup with the acrylic paint, both inside and outside, and leave to dry.
2. Stick the buttons around the rim of the cup and let dry.
3. Fill with shredded green tissue paper.

4. FINGER FLOWERS

These super-simple flowers are perfect to be given as a bunch or right inside the Fab Flowerpot above.

You Need:

• coloured pastel/chart paper • acrylic paint
• straws or sticks • scissors • white craft glue

MAKE IT!

1. Cut out simple rounded-petal flower shapes from pastel paper/chart paper.
2. Dip your finger into paint, dab off extra paint, then press down on each petal. Make a fingerprint with a contrasting colour in the centre of the flower.
3. Glue the straw/stick to the back of the flower.
4. Display the flowers in your Fab Flowerpot; or tie them in a bunch and present the bouquet to your mom.

5. MOM'S ENERGIZER

On Mother's Day or any weekend, take this super smoothie on a tray to mom—and lap up all the applause you get from her! It has no refined sugar, and is mellow and creamy.

You Need:

• 4 dates, pitted • 6 tablespoons museli
• 3/4 cup milk • 5 tablespoons plain yogurt
• pinch of cinnamom

MAKE IT!

1. Ask your dad or a grown-up to help—put all the ingredients in a blender, keeping aside one tablespoon of yogurt. Blend for at least 1 minute until smooth and creamy. Make sure all the muesli has been mixed in.
2. Pour into a glass, swirl in the spoonful of yogurt you kept aside and serve immediately.

6. HIGH-FIVE FOR MOM

Write a simple five-line poem called 'cinquain' for your mom. Have it framed.

You Need:

• paper • sketch pens

DO IT!

Here's how to do it:

Line 1: One word giving the title.
Line 2: Two words that describe the title.

Line 3: Three words that express action.
Line 4: Four words that express feeling.
Line 5: One word that gives the title a different name.

Here's an example:

Mommy
Tall, smiling
Working, caring, rushing
Magical healer, problem solver
Love.

7. DOOR BASKET

Surprise your mom with this quick-trick basket on the handle of her room door any day.

You Need:

• paper plate • scissors • sketch pens/paint/ kite paper • tape/stapler • hole punch • ribbon

MAKE IT!

1. Decorate the plate using sketch pens, paint or kite paper. Let it dry.
2. Now curl the paper plate into a cone shape. Tape or staple into place.
3. Punch two holes in the top of the cone, on opposite sides.

4. String a ribbon through the two holes, so you can hang the basket.
5. On a special day—Mother's Day, or your mom's birthday, or to say 'sorry' or 'thank you', fill the cone with real or handmade flowers. Hang on the door.

8. TWENTY WAYS

A mom by any other name is still as sweet! Here's how you can say 'mom' in 20 different languages.

	Language	Word	Say . . .
1.	Afrikaans	Moeder, Ma	*moh-duhr, maa*
2.	Albanian	Mëmë	*mum*
3.	Arabic	Ahm	*umm*
4.	Brazilian	Mãe	*may*
5.	Hawaiian	Makuahine	*mah-koo-ah-hee-nay*
6.	Czech	Majka	*mai-ka*
7.	Dutch	Moeder/Moer	*moe-duhr/mo-uhr*
8.	French	Mère, Maman	*mair/ma-moh*
9.	German	Mutter	*moo-tair*
10.	Greek	Màna	*mah-na*
11.	Indonesian	Ibu	*ee-boo*
12.	Italian	Madre/Mamma	*mah-dray/mah-mah*
13.	Japanese	Okasan	*oh-kaah-sahn*

14. Latin	Mater	*may-tuhr*
15. Mongolian	'Eh	*eh*
16. Persian	Madr	*mah-duhr*
17. Polish	Matka	*mat-kaa*
18. Russian	Maht'	*moh-ts*
19. Spanish	Madre	*mahd-ray*
20. Yiddish	Muter	*muh-ter*

9. MOM AND BABY BIRD

Your mom will absolutely love this little representation of a mother and her child—appreciation is guaranteed!

You Need!

- 2 baskets, one big and one small, plastic or cane
- four plastic flowers
- floral wire
- small piece of coloured foam
- 4 sturdy forked sticks (2 each of equal size)

MAKE IT!

1. Cut the stems off the plastic flowers. For each eye, fold a small length of floral wire in half and twist the loop end tightly around the flower. Position the flower on the bottom of the basket,

threading the ends of the wire through to the other side, then twist the ends to hold the eye in place.

2. To make each beak, cut a triangle shape from the foam, and use the wire to fix it to the basket.
3. For the feet, paint the sticks and allow them to dry. Place the sticks in the ground and keep a basket on each, securing it with the wire, if needed.

10. ROSE POTPOURRI

Potpourri is a French word (say *po-poo-ree*) and means 'fermented in a pot'. It's made with scented flowers, aromatic leaves and spices, and will make a great fragrant gift for your mom.

You Need:

• rose petals • 3 cinnamon sticks • a few drops of rose oil • two 4.5-inch squares of muslin or other breathable fabric • fabric glue/needle and thread

MAKE IT!

1. Lay rose petals out to dry on a flat surface for several days. You will need about 6 cups, so collect at least twice that many rose petals. Keep in a glass jar.
2. Add the cinnamon sticks and a few drops of scented oil. Mix. Shake every few days and let sit for 7–10 days.

3. Keep the two fabric pieces on top of each other and stick with the fabric glue or ask a grown-up to stitch it, leaving a small gap large enough to pour your potpourri through. Here's your sachet.

4. Fill the sachet with your chosen blend of potpourri. Avoid filling the bag too tightly.
5. Close up the gap. Keep the sachet in a pretty bag.

11. SUPER SILHOUETTE

A silhouette is an outline, usually black on a white background. Etienne de Silhouette, a Frenchman, was so good at it that all such pictures came to be known by his name. If Etienne could make them, you can too.

You Need:

• a room • a large sheet of white paper
• desk lamp • pencil • your mom

MAKE IT!

1. Stick (at the four corners) a large piece of white paper on a wall. Make your mother sit on a stool in front of it.
2. Light a desk lamp directed at your mom to create a sharp shadow on the paper. The closer the lamp is to her, the sharper her shadow will be on the wall. Have

your mother turn sideways. Tell her to sit still as a statue.

3. Use a pencil to draw an outline of your mother's head, neck and the top of her shoulders.
4. Reduce the outline on a photocopier and stick it on stiff black paper. Cut around the outline.
5. Turn it, black side up, and stick the silhouette on a white card. Draw a border round it. Gift it to your mom!

12. ALPHABET GAME

This is great when you are travelling with your mom or are out for a walk with her.

You need:

• your mom and yourself • topics
• presence of mind

PLAY IT!

1. Pick a topic and decide who will start the conversation.
2. Whoever starts talking (say, your mom) has to start their sentence with the letter A. Now you have to start

your sentence with the last letter of the last word of the sentence your mom just spoke.

3. Then she starts with the last letter of the last word you used in your sentence. This *antakshari* in prose is bound to be filled with lots of giggles. (You could exclude X from the game—and if a sentence ends with an X, use the letter just before it.)

13. FIFTY-FIFTY LOCKETS

Two lockets that come together to complete one message for your mom and you!

You Need:

• a small ball of wet clay • a craft knife • a compass
• two lengths of ribbon or two thin chains
• acrylic paints • clear varnish • paintbrush

MAKE IT!

1. Roll the clay into a circle and flatten it into a coin about 1 cm thick.
2. Using the compass, write a message across—for example: Mom & Me Forever.
3. Use the craft knife to make two halves from this one clay coin, making a zigzag cut down the middle.

4. Quickly make a hole at the top of each half—through which the ribbon/chain can pass.

5. Let the two halves of the clay coin dry. Paint the two lockets when dry.
6. Brush the lockets with varnish when the paint is dry.
7. Sting the ribbons/chains through the lockets. Give one locket to your mom to wear and keep the other one for yourself.

14. FAVOURITE THINGS

Your mom's most favourite things—all in one place! What could be better?

You Need:

• A-4 sized pastel sheet in your mom's favourite colour • pictures of your mom's favourite things: animals, birds, types of clothes, people, place to visit, actors, singers, gizmo and anything else you can think of • glue • cardboard

MAKE IT!

1. Cut out the pictures of your mother's favourite things from magazines and newspapers.

2. Arrange them on the pastel sheet, and when the composition looks good to you, start to stick the pictures down.
3. On a strip of paper, write 'Mom's Favourite Things', or cut out these words from a magazine/newspaper and stick them too. Let dry.
4. Now you can get it laminated as a special mat for your mom, or your mom can put it up as a poster.

15. MEMORIES BOARD

Your mom will love this board for memories of her and you together.

You Need:

• thick cardboard or softboard • self-adhesive paper, or gift wrap • rubber bands, elastic band, or narrow satin ribbon • piece of string • pair of scissors

MAKE IT!

1. Cover a 10–12 inch piece of cardboard with brightly coloured self-adhesive paper, or gift wrap.
2. Cut several small slits along each side of the cardboard. Stretch different coloured rubber bands, or elastic bands across the board, inserting them in the slits, to make a crisscross design. You can also do this

with ribbons, making sure they are tightly stretched and tightly secured or knotted at the back.

3. To hang up the bulletin board, make a loop by threading a piece of yarn through two holes at the top and tying the ends together.
4. Slide in reminders, cards and photographs under the rubber band/elastic band/ribbon. Gift it to your mom.

16. NO-COOK POPS

Ask a grown-up to help you make these banana pops for your mom—and then you can share the recipe with her. And you can let her choose her favourite 'coating'.

You Need:

• 2 bananas • 4 ice-cream sticks • 1 chocolate bar • 1 tbsp. chopped nuts, crispy rice cereal, or shredded coconut • butter knife • waxed paper

MAKE IT!

1. Peel the bananas and remove any stringy fibre. Cut the bananas in half, widthwise, and push an ice-cream stick through the cut end of each half.

2. Cover them in cling-wrap and freeze for three hours.
4. Ask a grown-up to melt the chocolate bar in a microwave on high for about 2 minutes, or heat in a pan. Stir in the nuts, cereal, or coconut.
5. Using a butter knife, spread the chocolate mixture over the frozen bananas to coat them completely. Keep the pops on a plate covered with waxed paper and freeze until ready to serve. *Makes 4 pops.*

17. MESSAGE BOTTLE

A cool way to package a message, a poem, a drawing, or a letter to your mom.

You Need:

• unusually shaped glass bottles with a lid or preferably cork, for a quaint look • ribbon • heart shapes cut out from pastel paper • aquarium rocks (the glass ones) • sequins or coloured pebbles or beads • a message for your mom (as a small card or on paper)

MAKE IT!

5. Clean the glass bottles and dry them.
6. Put the aquarium rocks/coloured pebbles, sequins/beads to fill up one-third of the bottle. Then keep two card hearts on top.

7. Roll up your message and put it inside the bottle.
8. Tie a ribbon on the bottle.

18. WOW WRAPPING

Wrap a gift for your mom in fancied-up newspaper and get a pat on your shoulder for recycling.

You Need:

• old newspapers (choose happy pages, not those with tragic news) • sponge and poster paint/ stickers/chocolate foil or candy wrappers/ old artifcial flowers/ribbons

MAKE IT!

1. If you look carefully, you might find a page that matches your gift or gives a clue to it. Say, if you have a painting kit, and there's an article about a painter, use that page.
2. Or you can dab colour with a sponge to brighten up the paper. Old stickers work well too. Or cut out any pictures from calendars and paste them. Once you have wrapped the gift, make small flowers with candy wrappers (fold like a fan, fold into half and tape it down) or chocolate foil and tape them on.
3. Stick articial flowers on top and tie a big bow.

19. HAND HOLDER

A funky jewellery holder for your mom's rings, necklaces and bracelets.

You Need:

• a rubber glove in a bright colour • a tall, glass bottle • pebbles, preferably coloured, to fill into the glass bottle, or acrylic paints • stuffing, such as polyfill from an old pillow/cottonwool

MAKE IT!

1. Fill the glove with stuffing so that it looks like a 'real' hand, up to the 'wrist' area.
2. Fill the glass bottle with coloured pebbles or decorate it with a bright design, using acrylic paints.
3. Pull the glove down the length of the glass bottle.
4. Yay! The jewellery holder is ready. Now you can add some rings and things to it.

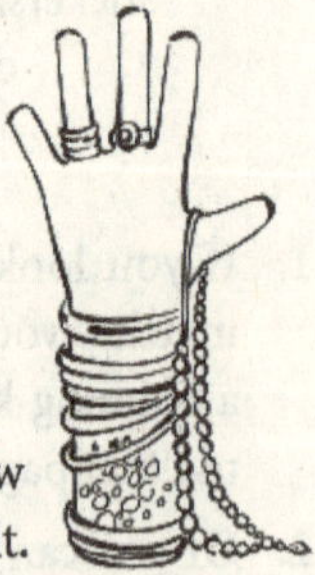

20. FOLLOW MY FINGER

A forgotten but fun game—revive it with your mom.

You Need:

- severeal pieces of paper (A-4 size will do)
- pen/pencil • any objects (without sharp edges)

PLAY IT!

One of you closes her eyes and offers your non-dominant hand (the one you don't use to write), in the fully open position, to the other person, who takes it, palm down, guides it gently over the object, while the other person, with eyes closed, proceeds to use her free hand to draw the object. Try it—it has weird and wonderful results!

21. BOOKMARKS

These bookmarks will be a hit with your mom!

You Need:

- pastel paper in different colours • sketch pens
- narrow ribbons in different colours • craft glue

MAKE IT!

1. Cut heart shapes from pastel paper. Make a design on them with sketch pens.
2. Cut a length of ribbon about 7 inches long. Keeping it between the two heart pieces, stick the hearts together.

3. Now cut three smaller bits of ribbon and stick them on the long ribbon, one below the other. Your bookmark is ready!

22. JUNK SCULPTURE

Great for some unwinding on spring-cleaning day. First help your mom tidy up, then do this together.

You Need:

• Household junk: anyting goes, such as cardboard boxes, plastic spoons and forks, tin foil, bags, straws, toothpicks, plastic bottles, small toys...

DO IT!

1. Give yourself 2 minutes to collect whatever junk you can from a carton. Discard breakable or sharp objects.
2. Now create a steady sculpture, using the junk you collected. Get another family member or neighbour/friend to judge whose is more creative!

23. MOMMY OATH

You Need:

• paper/pastel paper • sketch pens • aluminium foil or little scraps of coloured paper • your head

MAKE IT!

1. On a sheet of paper, write down ten promises to your mom—everything from 'I will finish everything on my plate' to 'I will tidy my cupboards every two months'... Make sure they're promises that you will keep.
2. Now decorate the paper with a design or border or with foil or little scraps. Have it framed and gift it to your mom.

24. GIFT BASKET

A special basket for your mom's hankies and knick-knacks and other small things.

You Need:

• small plastic or cane basket • crepe paper streamers, ribbon, or strips of fabric (the length of your arm) • a plastic flower

MAKE IT!

1. Fold strips of crêpe paper streamers/ribbons lengthwise in half, reducing the width.
2. Weave the streamer/ribbon/ fabric strip through the holes, anyway you want. For a bow, start weaving from the middle of one side of the basket, with

the middle of the ribbon. Weave one half, then the other and stop at the opposite side, and tie a bow.

3. Tie a streamer/ribbon/fabric strip around the handle.
4. Twist the stem of a plastic flower through a few holes.
5. Fill the basket with whatever you like.

25. MOMS ARE THE BEST!

Write your favourite mommy quotes here.

1. *God could not be everywhere and therefore he made mothers.* —Jewish Proverb
2. --
